DEMYSTIFYING WALL STREET

The Investor's Guide to Stock Market Timing

ROY E. SANDSTROM

Dearborn
Financial Publishing, Inc.

Dedication

This book is dedicated to my wife, Judy, and my daughter, Joanna, who are a source of both joy and inspiration.

Publisher: Kathleen A. Welton
Associate Editor: Karen A. Christensen
Senior Project Editor: Jack L. Kiburz
Interior Design: Lucy Jenkins
Cover Design: Mary Kushmir

Printed in the United States of America

92 93 94 10 9 8 7 6 5 4 3 2 1

Library of Congress Cataloging-in-Publication Data

Sandstrom, Roy E.
    Demystifying Wall Street : the investor's guide to stock market timing / Roy E. Sandstrom.
       p. cm.
    Includes bibliographical references (p.) and index.
    ISBN 0-79310-374-6
    1. Stocks. 2. Investments. I. Title.
HG4661.S27 1992
332.63'22—dc20

92-257
CIP

Contents

Chapter 5 • Sentiment   54

Chapter 6 • Charts and Moving Averages   69

Chapter 9 • Reading the Tea Leaves: Some Indirect Evidence

Figures/Tables List

FIGURES

TABLES

Preface

When I first began to study the stock market, I knew little about investments of any kind. Like most people, I felt embarrassed over my ignorance. Seeking help from my friends, I discovered that few of them really understood the stock or bond markets or could offer any substantial advice.

I went to the public and university libraries in my hometown and read everything I could find. At first, I read uncritically, absorbing information like a sponge, good advice with the bad. I read financial columns in local newspapers and watched financial programs on television. After awhile, I became very confused. Every day, experts were predicting that the stock market would move up sharply, decline sharply or "stay in a trading range"—whatever that meant. The books I read made all kinds of claims for specific trading systems that could make you a lot of money, while other books argued that there was no way to consistently beat the market averages.

Unable to resolve that dispute for myself, I subscribed to a series of relatively inexpensive advisory newsletters that provided information geared to the no-load mutual fund investor. Like most average investors, I read *Money* magazine and watched financial news programs on CNN and CNBC/FNN as well as "Wall Street Week" on public television. Finally, I started reading *The Wall Street Journal* and *Barron's*, two financial journals that are filled with interesting articles and useful statistics.

Undaunted by the crash of 1987, I continued to read about technical analysis, to gather data and to follow the market. Over time, I found some basic timing models and trading systems that seemed to beat a buy-and-hold strategy. In this book, I have tried to focus on some of the most promising technical indicators and to offer cautionary remarks on those that look good on the surface but that may be seriously flawed. What follows is a detailed commentary on various aspects of technical analysis and market-timing. With due apologies to those who believe in Elliott waves, Kondratiev cycles, Fibonacci numbers and astrology, I have tried to avoid systems and methods that seem to be fraught with superstition, numerology, astrology, metaphysics or poor research.

The average investor is bombarded with all types of claims for stock-market newsletters and market-timing systems that supposedly generate huge profits. While some of these publications and systems are extremely worthwhile, an enormous amount of junk is being peddled to average investors. Over the course of my research, I discovered some principles that seemed to make great sense as well as some market-timing models that actually work. I wanted to write this book to share some of these insights with people very much like myself.

The Glossary contains definitions of technical terms used in the text. When a technical term is introduced for the first time but is not defined in the text itself, it has been highlighted to direct the reader to the Glossary. The Bibliography contains a list of some of the best books I read in the process of my research. The chapter endnotes contain both documentation of specific points and additional information for experienced investors. Appendix III lists the raw data from which my calculations were made. Thus, if you have the time and the patience, you can verify the claims made for my timing model in Chapter 12.

I remain convinced that there are many successful investment strategies. What works for one person may not work for another. In this book, I have tried to offer a variety of alternatives that make sense for ordinary investors engaged in other full-time professional work. Thus, the focus in this book is on intermediate-term to long-term market-timing systems rather than on short-term systems that are better suited for full-time professional investors.

Acknowledgments

Several individuals helped to make this book possible and deserve special recognition. I want to thank especially my wife, Judy, for her support and confidence in my work. Without her encouragement, this book never would have been finished. I also want to thank those who read early drafts of the manuscript and made many helpful suggestions. These include Lawrence Kieffer, Robert Morgan, Robert Neymeyer, Charles Quirk, Neal Siebert and Kevin Wedeking.

Charles Strein deserves special thanks for the hours he spent discussing various ideas contained in this manuscript during their embryonic stage. Gene Lutz provided invaluable advice on statistical and methodological issues raised by my research. I also want to thank Lyle Bowlin for helping me with some of the more complex technical issues associated with this project.

Introduction

Most people approach investing with a mixture of fear and greed. The stock market crash of 1987 and the almost daily revelations of insider trading and illegal activities by stockbrokers created great concern about the safety and integrity of the stock market. Program trading has frightened many conservative **investors**. There are countless stories of dishonest brokers defrauding widows and orphans. Insider-trading scandals abound. No one seems to be able to consistently time the market, selling high and buying low. Some experts always are telling the investor that now is the perfect time to be buying stocks, while other equally famous people are telling you to sell everything to avoid catastrophe.

No wonder the small investor is confused and tends to find safety in broadly diversified mutual funds and in long-term buy-and-hold strategies such as dollar cost averaging. Unfortunately, such strategies produce mediocre results. Is there a better alternative?

Some experts claim that it is possible to beat the broader market averages and to produce superior returns through either stock picking, market timing or a combination of both. This text is written for individuals who are willing to take risks and to actively trade stocks or mutual funds and who hope that, within the realm of technical analysis, there may be some secrets that will enhance their chances of accumulating greater wealth.

THE HUMAN FACTOR

Our personalities and our emotions affect the way we invest. Many people are intimidated by the stock market and prefer passive investment strategies that require little thinking on their part. They are likely to adopt one approach to investment early in their lives and stay with it through thick and thin. Although their money is at risk, they refuse to take responsibility for their financial future. If you are that type of person, you have my sympathy, but this book is not for you. This book is intended, instead, for people who have the courage to make financial decisions and who want greater profits from their stock-market investments.

Some people are optimists; others are pessimists. Some have enormous self-confidence; others are quite timid. Each of these personality types tends to behave quite differently. Each of us must identify the types of investments and investment strategies that are appropriate for ourselves. Eternal optimists tend to see nothing but record profits and soaring stock-market prices ahead. While these people are likely to profit from the long-term, upward bias in the stock market, they also are prone to buy at the very top of a market rally. Perennial pessimists believe that another great depression and stock market crash are just around the corner. These people are likely to invest in bonds rather than stocks, and if they have any stocks at all, they also are prone to sell them at a major market bottom. Others may not know where the economy or stock market is going but are afraid that, whatever happens, they will get hurt. These people are unlikely to take a very active role in their investments. By the time that they have the courage to invest, the **bull market** is likely to be over. By the time they finally decide to sell, the ultimate bottom of the **bear market** probably is in sight. Some unfortunate investors are so driven by greed that they want to squeeze every last dollar (and cent) out of their investments and will ride a speculative investment to the brink of catastrophe. These people also are likely to overtrade, generating large commissions for their brokers.

Individual investor psychology limits what we can hope to achieve with our investments. Each of us has had conditioning experiences that affect the way we regard wealth, risk and the markets. Knowing yourself and your attitude toward risk is one of the most important single characteristics of a sound investment strategy. Developing a disciplined investment strategy is an extremely important key to successful investment without undue stress. The more experience you have in following the markets and the more you buy and sell stocks or mutual funds, the more knowledge (and confidence) you will develop.

INVESTMENT ALTERNATIVES

Most individual investors should avoid futures, options, options on futures, commodities and other highly leveraged or extremely volatile investments. For some investors, collectibles (such as rare coins, stamps, antique furniture, baseball cards or art) may have an appeal. These investments, however, often lack liquidity, i.e., they are hard to sell when you want or need to sell them. The difference between the bid and the ask price, i.e., between what the buyer offers and what the seller demands, may be considerable. Thus, you often may buy high and sell low.

For most people, fixed-income and growth-oriented investments are much more appropriate. Within the fixed-income category, investors can choose between corporate, federal, state and municipal bonds; mortgage-backed securities; certificates of deposit; money market accounts; and passbook savings accounts. Within the growth-oriented investment category, investors can choose between real estate, common and preferred stocks and mutual funds. While fixed-income investments provide stability and security of current income, they do so at the expense of slow capital appreciation. While growth-oriented investments provide greater long-term capital appreciation, they do so at the expense of short-term income.

For those who seek highly liquid investments with excellent prospects for long-term capital appreciation, common stocks are extremely attractive. Many investors buy stocks in companies recommended by brokers, friends or financial commentators. In theory, you want to buy stocks in companies with good management, excellent product lines, an expanding market share and good balance sheets. In any case, the decision-making criteria used by investors to select individual stocks fall into one of two major categories: fundamental analysis or technical analysis.

FUNDAMENTAL ANALYSIS

Fundamental analysis is the study of the profitability of a specific firm, industry or market based on corporate financial data. Fundamental analysts study such things as quarterly and annual reports to find information on corporate sales, revenues, operating profits, earnings, debt, inventory, cash flow, etc. For the average investor who wants to create a portfolio of stocks to purchase and hold for long-term capital appreciation, fundamental analysis makes great sense. It is, however, very demanding and time-consuming work.

TECHNICAL ANALYSIS

Technical analysis sometimes is defined as the mathematical study of stock prices. That definition, however, is too restrictive. Technical analysis usually involves the study of a wide range of both stock market and macroeconomic data, including such things as the number of stocks advancing or declining, the number of stocks hitting 52-week new highs or new lows, the volume in advancing shares, the volume in declining shares and the total volume. Many technical analysts also pay close attention to aggregate statistics on corporate earnings, dividends, interest rates, money supply, job growth, inflation, etc., in their analysis. This list could be expanded to include bank reserves, credit, consumer debt, capacity utilization, employment growth and trade deficits.

LONG-TERM INVESTMENT VERSUS SHORT-TERM TRADING

Financial experts often advise the average investor to invest for the long run, to buy and hold stocks or mutual funds for several years or more to allow for long-term growth in the broader economy to push up stock prices. This makes excellent sense and is good advice for most people. But other financial experts tout short-term trading systems that supposedly offer the prospect of superior returns on your investment.

Which approach is best? Is it possible to improve your returns on your investments through more timely purchases and sales of stocks or mutual funds? Cynics argue that many technical trading systems work well for a while and then fail miserably. Once the investing public learns about a trading system, it no longer may work because others anticipate its rules and thus invalidate them. Simple models eventually may fail because something happens to invalidate the underlying assumptions of that model. Complex models may fail because the inclusion of multiple indicators creates redundancy rather than progressively higher levels of accuracy. Statisticians point out that including a large number of **dummy variables** will strengthen a regression equation despite the fact that such variables represent **random noise.** Some trading systems are too dependent on a particular set of data. (Technicians often refer to this as excessive curve fitting.) Pure trading systems can be savaged by unexpected economic events, while systems based on macoeconomic indicators provide only general orientation to the market, not precise buy-and-sell signals.

Even the skeptics agree, however, that it is possible to generate superior returns—if you devote sufficient time and effort to develop a high level of expertise. This book is intended to shorten that initial effort from several years to a few months. It is intended for average investors with a limited amount of time to spend studying the stock and bond markets who prefer to invest in no-load mutual funds and make investment decisions every few weeks or months. How well you ultimately succeed depends on your talent, effort and luck.

1

Realistic Financial Planning

Before you plunge too deeply into the stock market or become infatuated with technical analysis and stock market timing, you must sit back and engage in some sensible, long-term financial planning. Whether your goals are to ensure a safe and secure retirement or to provide for your children's education, you must identify these goals and take a long, hard look at what kind of investment strategy meets your personal needs. Many people need expert advice at this stage to develop a long-term plan for the future. If so, you might seek the help of a financial planner.

CERTIFIED FINANCIAL PLANNERS

A number of national organizations of financial planners exists and every medium-sized community has one or more full-time, professional money managers to help you with your investments. You might ask your banker or attorney to help you find a fee-based, certified financial planner who does not sell investment products. Be careful if you use a planner who sells products on commission. This creates a potential conflict of interest between the planner's roles as adviser and salesperson. You might contact the National Association of Personal Financial Advisors (1130 Lake Cook Road, Buffalo Grove, IL 60089) for the name of someone in your area. Ask that planner to choose a broadly diversified no-load mutual fund family that has a series of indexed funds, a money market account and a variety of fixed-income accounts.

Most mutual fund families include specific funds that track one or more of the major indexes, including the Major Market Index (XMI), the Dow Jones Industrial Average (DJIA), the Standard and Poor's 100 (S&P 100), the Standard and Poor's 500 (S&P 500), the Value Line Index, the Russell 2,000 or the National Association of Securities Dealers Automated Quotation Composite Index (the NASDAQ Composite Index). You want a fund family that offers three different levels of choice, e.g., the XMI or the DJIA, the S&P 100 or the S&P 500 and the Value Line or the NASDAQ. On the fixed-income side, you want that company to offer short-term, intermediate-term and long-term government bond funds as well. It would be helpful if that company also had a municipal bond fund and a corporate bond fund that invested in bonds rated AA or higher.

Once you have chosen an appropriate no-load mutual fund family that offers a variety of investment alternatives, ask your planner to develop an asset-allocation strategy that is appropriate for your needs. This consists of determining how much money should be invested in various types of funds, including real estate investment trusts (REITs), stock funds, bond funds, money-market funds, precious metals funds, etc.

DIVERSIFICATION

The efficient market school recommends diversification to reduce investment risk. Thus, if stocks do poorly, bonds, real estate, precious metals or Treasury bills might do better. Real estate, cash and precious metals are excellent hedges against rapid inflation, while stocks and bonds do well in a stable or declining interest-rate environment. In a rare deflationary environment, cash is king. For the risk-averse investor, diversification into stocks, bonds and cash is an excellent strategy that reduces the **volatility** of your portfolio. Thus, while markets may gyrate, your net worth will remain much more stable.

REAL ESTATE

Many Americans have long thought that their homes are excellent forms of investment. More recently, however, those who have tried to sell their homes during a housing slump have realized that cyclical patterns of boom and bust in the housing industry add to the problems of illiquidity of this investment. In some parts of the country, houses have appreciated rapidly with every passing year. In other parts of the country, house prices have stagnated for a decade or more. Thus, from an investment standpoint, a private home carries a series of hidden risks.

When financial experts recommend that 33 percent of your total assets should be in real estate, they usually are talking about a combination of your home along with other real estate investments, including land, shopping centers, condominiums, commercial buildings, etc. Obviously, it is hard for individuals to participate in the real estate market in any area other than their own region. For that reason, advisers recommend REITs, especially those that invest in property rather than in mortgages. One method for choosing REITs seems to possess considerable merit.

James Kuhle and Josef Morehead developed a complex formula for selecting a REIT. They based their system on six indicators, which they described in detail in an article in *The Wall Street Journal*. The specifics of the model need not concern us here; the approach is what is significant. The authors used data available from *Standard and Poor's Stock Guide* and *The Value Line Investment Survey:* dividend yield, the price-earnings ratio, the price-to-book ratio, the debt-to-equity ratio, earnings growth and diversification of holdings.

According to this article, only 20 REITs out of 102 actively traded between 1977 and 1985 passed all six tests. However, those 20 REITs had an "average annual return of 31%, nearly twice the S&P 500's 16.8% average annual return over the same period."[1] Critics of this system point out that an investor also should look at operating cash flow to adjust for depreciation.

REITs not only make great sense within a diversified portfolio, but also a system such as the one discussed above might prove to be an appropriate screening method. Unfortunately, many investors find the Kuhle/Morehead method too complicated. In fact, the use of a relative strength indicator (described in Chapter 7) is a simple and effective method that could be used by most investors for picking out REITs.

FINANCIAL ASSETS

The remaining two-thirds of your total assets are your financial assets. Only a small fraction of your financial assets—5 to 10 percent—should be in precious metals, with the rest divided between stocks and bonds. The actual division of your assets between stocks and bonds, however, ought to be based not only on your aversion to risk but also on the number of years before you plan to retire.

RETIREMENT PLANNING

Many people are far too exposed to the stock market for their own good. When you are in your 20s or 30s, it makes good sense to take greater risks with your portfolio and to include in it a larger percentage of stocks or other high-volatility, high-capital-growth, low-yield investments. As you approach retirement age, however, you must scale down these riskier, more volatile investments and seek instead less volatile, more predictable investments. It is dangerous to wait too long and then abruptly transfer all of your assets from stocks to bonds as you get close to retirement. You might, for example, find yourself in the midst of a severe bear market and your stocks may have lost a substantial part of their value.

On the other hand, some investors are exposed too much to the fixed-income market. Inflation can eat away the real value of your investments, leaving you worse off with each passing year. To balance the need for portfolio stability against risks of inflation, you might want to consider an asset-allocation formula based on age to retirement.

AGE TO RETIREMENT

Regardless of whether a certified financial planner designs an asset-allocation strategy to meet your own personal needs or you decide to do it yourself, one vital ingredient in any such plan should be the number of years before you plan to retire. Table 1.1 offers one example of how such an asset-allocation system might be constructed.

STOCKS VERSUS MUTUAL FUNDS

Once you have determined what percentage of your financial assets should be devoted to stocks, you must decide between individual stocks and mutual funds. If you decide to buy individual stocks, you will have to be a very active investor and spend a great deal of time studying individual companies or you will have to rely on professional advice.

BROKERS

Unfortunately, there is no way to know how good (or bad) the advice of stockbrokers may be for brokerages do not submit their

TABLE 1.1   Age to Retirement

Years to Retirement	Fixed Income	Stock Funds
40	0%	100%
35	10	90
30	20	80
25	30	70
20	40	60
15	50	50
10	60	40
5	70	30
0	75	25

records to independent audit. Investors also have to be concerned about the churning of accounts, i.e., excessive commissions generated through too-frequent trading. One of the more shocking accounts of the way that customers can be fleeced by brokers is contained in Michael Lewis's controversial book, *Liar's Poker*. Even if only 10 percent of the stories in Lewis's book were true, investors would have good reason to exercise extreme caution when dealing with brokers.

You must remember that brokers primarily are salespeople who have a vested interest in convincing others to trade stocks. Thus, stockbrokers' advice has a healthy element of self-interest and should be regarded with some skepticism. There may well be many honest and talented brokers, but getting good advice never is easy. The problem is to avoid bad advice or an unscrupulous adviser. What is perhaps even worse is that the average broker has many demands made on his time and has to rely on the quality of research conducted by the parent organization. That means that the expertise you might expect may not be available at a local office.

Some brokerages seem perennially optimistic and consistently recommend investing high percentages of your total assets in stocks. Unfortunately, many analysts are overworked and pressured to develop positive recommendations for specific firms. Analysts also have a herd mentality and tend to confirm one another's estimates. For example, in March of 1991, most analysts had expected IBM's earnings to be approximately $1.80 per share for the first quarter. These analysts were understandably surprised when the company announced that earnings would be approximately half that level. Remember, this is for the largest stock in many portfolios, for a company that is followed widely, in an industry that has a very high public visibility.

You also must be aware of the way some firms use language. Thus, a "strong buy" might mean "buy the stock." A "weak buy" can mean "hold the stock." A "hold" recommendation could mean "sell the stock."

MARKET ADVISORY SERVICES

Because it is so hard to time the purchase or sale of stocks or mutual funds by yourself, you might think about subscribing to a leading market newsletter. Just be careful. It is very hard to get reliable data on these newsletters. In some cases, the publisher may send insufficient information for you to make an informed decision. You need at least five years of performance data along with a comparison of those results to the S&P 500.

Some market advisers have excellent long-term records, but the media darlings of one year may not be the most consistent performers. Joe Granville used to be the hottest market timer around. From 1982 to 1986, however, Granville remained bearish in the face of a strong bull market. But again in 1988, he rose to the top of the charts and continued to have a hot hand well into 1991. Similarly, Al Frank was one of the top stock pickers for the past bull market, but his heavy use of margin buying magnified his losses during the crash. More recently, he has recovered his excellent performance rating. He even got his subscribers out before the minicrash of 1989.

Perhaps the best example of a recent media star is Robert Prechter whose Elliott Wave Theory eludes systematic testing. Prechter, a fine technical analyst, was the hottest stock market forecaster during 1982-1987. He gave a sell signal on the eve of the 1987 crash. But he remained bearish afterward while the market rallied 1,000 points. Obviously, stock-market gurus can run hot and then cold over time.

Personally, I enjoy the comments of a great number of analysts, including Charles Allmon, Tom Aspray, Roy Blumberg, John Bollinger, Craig Corcoran, Mike Drakulich, Lynn Elgert, Peter Eliades, A. J. Frost, Justin Mamis, R. B. McCurtain, John Murphy, Robert Nurock, Robert Prechter, Philip Roth, Russ Wassendorf, Stan Weinstein and Martin Zweig. These and other familiar faces on CNBC/FNN, "Money Line" and "Wall Street Week" enjoy long records of success and have a great deal of experience and wisdom to share with the public. You can learn a lot from the famous market gurus. What they say, however, has to be regarded as simply informed opinion and must be evaluated on its own merits. Chapter 5 discusses the dangers of "group think" in considerable detail and concludes that when all the experts agree, they are most likely to be dead wrong!

Unfortunately, relatively few of these experts had their subscribers out of the stock market by 16 October 1987, the last trading day before the crash.[2] Additionally, few had their clients' portfolios heavily in cash by the end of September, a time when the market was beginning to disintegrate. Some letters (e.g., Richard Russell's *Dow Theory Letters*, James Stack's *Investech* newsletter, Martin Zweig's *Zweig Forecast* and Stan Weinstein's *Professional Tape Reader*), however, did have their readers heavily in cash by 30 September 1987, a date that allowed their readers sufficient time to receive the newsletters, absorb their contents and make the transfers or sales required.

An ideal scenario would have been to be heavily invested until the end of August, less fully invested by 30 September and largely in cash by 16 October. Over these three periods, Russell had his clients 100, 0 and 0 percent invested, respectively. Stack had his 42, 12 and 0 percent invested. Zweig's clients were 50, 29 and 10 percent invested. Weinstein's clients were 51, 36 and 11 percent invested on those three dates. As a group, these four gurus had their readers 61 percent invested on 31 August, 19 percent invested on 30 September and 5 percent invested on 16 October (see Table 1.2).

Someone following their collective advice and invested in a mutual fund indexed to the S&P 500 would have lost approximately 4.6 percent from 2 October 1987 to 23 October 1987 (when the S&P 500 dropped from 328.07 to 248.22) versus a 24.3 percent loss for someone fully invested. These results for 1987 seem quite impressive. On the other hand, only Zweig seems to have been consistently bullish in the 1988–1989 period. Thus, short-term performance rankings for market newsletters may be misleading.

A number of excellent market letters are available. Consult *The Individual Investor's Guide to Investment Publications*, 1st ed., 1988, for names and addresses as well as a brief description of each letter. Also, be sure to consult Mark Hulbert's, *The Hulbert Guide to Financial Newsletters*, 4th ed., 1991. When you write to a newsletter publisher, ask for sample copies from the publisher of the newsletter along with a five-year performance report comparing that newsletter's results to the S&P 500.

If a newsletter has a long-term record of success and a good **risk-adjusted return**, it is worth considering. According to the *Hulbert Financial Digest*,[3] the top market letters for the period 30 June 1980 to 31 December 1990 in terms of total return were the *Zweig Forecast* (+492.9 percent), the *Value Line Investment Survey* (+419.5 percent), the *Growth Stock Outlook* (+363.4 percent) and the *Chartist*

TABLE 1.2   Expert Market Timing in 1987 (Percent Invested)

Name	*31 August*	*30 September*	*16 October*
Russell	100%	0%	0%
Stack	42	12	0
Zweig	50	29	10
Weinstein	51	36	11
Average	61	19	5

(+352.1 percent), which all beat the total return on the Wilshire 5,000 (+302.8 percent).

ADVANTAGES OF MUTUAL FUNDS

For many investors, the time and effort required to follow individual stocks is prohibitive. For these investors, mutual funds offer several advantages. With mutual funds, you are hiring a full-time professional to choose individual stocks and to manage your portfolio. Mutual funds provide much better diversification across various industries and among different companies than is possible for the average investor with relatively small sums of money to invest. Mutual funds also buy stocks in large blocks. As a result, they benefit from low commission costs. The average individual can invest small sums of money on a regular basis with mutual funds, whereas small stock purchases result in high commission costs. For an individual with less than $15,000 to invest, mutual funds make particularly good sense. A serious question, however, is whether you should pay a sales commission or an exit fee for the privilege of buying a specific mutual fund.

LOAD FUNDS

Some stockbrokers claim that their mutual funds that charge a load or sales commission[4] outperform **no-load funds**. They insist that you receive superior expertise with these funds and that no-load funds don't deliver the same performance. Actually, the 3 to 8 percent load is a sales commission. None of this money goes into the analysis of stocks or the market. Thus, the load fee does not affect the quality of stock selection. All it does is reduce your initial investment. Research suggests that it takes about 15 years for the typical 8 percent load fund to equal the total returns of the average no-load fund because of the loss of initial investment capital due to commission costs. Put simply, an investor with $1,000 to invest starts out with $1,000 in a no-load fund versus $920 in an 8 percent load fund. That disadvantage takes a long time to overcome.

Some other funds claim that they are no-load funds, but actually charge an exit or redemption fee at the time of sale. This is another form of load fund. On the other hand, if a load fund has a long-term record of superior performance and if it still has the same manager, it might be worth considering. As a rule, it takes eight years to recover from a front-end load of 8 percent if the load fund experiences a 1 percent excess return per year over the broader market averages. It takes more than five years to recover that cost if the fund has an excess return of 1.5 percent per year and only four years if the excess return is 2 percent per year.

NO-LOAD MUTUAL FUNDS

For most investors, no-load mutual funds make good sense. A great number of diversified, no-load mutual funds are available. You should look for true no-load funds that do not charge commissions or exit fees. Preferably, a no-load fund should not charge an advertising fee, called a 12b-1. Also, that fund should charge a low management fee ranging from 0.5 percent to no more than 1 percent of current assets. Look for funds that are based on some familiar index such as the S&P 500's list of 500 large capitalization stocks or the NASDAQ. That way, the fund's performance will be a function of changes in that index, adjusted for the percentage of cash the fund holds and the management fees it charges.

DOLLAR COST AVERAGING

In view of fairly substantial evidence in favor of market efficiency and the difficulties in finding an honest broker or a good stock-market analyst, most small investors might be much better off to use a no-load mutual fund indexed to the S&P 500 as an investment vehicle. Don't try to time the stock market. Just put a specific amount of money into stocks each month (or quarter). If the market is expensive, you will buy fewer shares of that fund. If the market is inexpensive, you will buy more shares with the same amount of money. Over time, this system reduces the costs of purchasing stock. When you need to sell your shares, sell a portion of your total each month as you dollar cost average out of the market. This combination of dollar cost averaging and buy and hold should maximize your total returns. This method makes excellent sense and should represent the basic strategy of most investors.

MUTUAL FUND SELECTION

If, on the other hand, you hope to achieve better-than-average returns, you must take a more active role in determining your financial future. Choose mutual funds that have enjoyed superior performance over several time periods, e.g., one year, five years and ten years. Make sure that the fund still has the same manager. If you select new funds, be sure that the manager has a long-term record of success, e.g., someone like Peter Lynch, John Neff, Milton Berg, Richard Fontaine, Al Frank, John Templeton or Martin Zweig. If performance is random as some academicians claim, you will not hurt your chances of success simply because the success (or failure) of a mutual fund in one year supposedly has no bearing on how it will do in a subsequent year. On the other hand, if the pessimists are wrong, then you will be employing a strategy that has some prospect of identifying a mutual fund that has a chance of superior performance.

A more sophisticated strategy for choosing no-load mutual funds was developed by Dr. Gary Zin.[5] Zin suggests that an investor should select no-load mutual funds that have been consistently in the top 20 percent of all no-load funds for the past three months. Choose the five at the top of that list and diversify your money among all five. Sell any one of them when it falls below the top 20 percent level. According to Zin, this should result in a 33 percent excess return over the S&P 500. If Zin is correct, this is perhaps the optimal strategy for most active investors, just as dollar cost averaging is the optimal strategy for most passive investors.

One excellent source of information on the performance of mutual funds is *Growth Fund Guide,* which provides performance reports for no-load mutual funds for the past 3, 6, 9 and 12 months. Another very useful source of information is *Investor's Business Daily,* which publishes relative strength rankings and information about the performance of specific mutual-fund groups.

HOW MUCH RISK?

There always is a trade-off between risk and reward. Under normal conditions, the greater the safety of an investment, the lower the rate of return. The higher the risk, the greater the reward. Thus, junk bonds pay a higher rate of interest than safer Treasury bonds. (The collapse of the junk-bond market in late 1989 convinced many investors that high returns came at the price of safety and liquidity.) But this does not mean that wild speculative gambles pay off. The risk-reward relationship is curvilinear and moderate risk makes sense. High risk does not. The ability to sleep well at night is a vital element in any successful investment program. If you find yourself too concerned about the safety of your portfolio, you probably need to stress safety of principal above all else.

REALISTIC EXPECTATIONS

You must have realistic expectations. Over the past 60 years, the stock market has returned approximately 10 percent per year, while inflation averaged about 4 percent for a real return of 6 percent. To determine the rate at which your money will double its value, divide 72 by the rate of interest. At a 6 percent rate, you will double the real value of your investment every 12 years. While you might hope for

TABLE 1.3   Long-Term Returns on Investments

Category	*Returns*
Small company stocks	$219.90
Common stocks	60.47
Corporate bonds	3.26
Treasury bonds	2.18
Treasury bills	1.33

SOURCE: *Stocks, Bonds, Bills, and Inflation 1989 Yearbook™*, Ibbotson Associates, Chicago (annually updates work by Roger G. Ibbotson and Rex A. Sinquefield). All Rights Reserved.

more than that, experience suggests that an inflation-adjusted gain of 6 percent per year is a good rate of return and anything better than that will take considerable effort, knowledge or luck on your part. Avoid people who promise investment vehicles or strategies that will guarantee a 30 percent or more return per year. Those kinds of claims almost always are fraudulent or conceal a very high level of risk.

Table 1.3 reflects what happened to the inflation-adjusted total returns for one dollar invested in small company stocks, common stocks, long-term corporate bonds, Treasury bonds and Treasury bills from 1925 to 1988.

Obviously, the long-term, inflation-adjusted total returns for both small company and common stocks far outstrip the performance of both bills and bonds.

BETA

When you select mutual funds, pay attention to the beta. The beta is a measure of the relationship between the price of a stock (or fund) and that of the broader market. By definition, the beta of the S&P 500 is 1.0. Mutual funds whose prices rise (or decline) faster than the S&P 500 have betas greater than 1.0. Funds whose prices rise (or decline) less rapidly than the S&P 500 have betas below 1.0. Differences in beta are a function of the relative volatility of the portfolios chosen by mutual-fund managers and the amount of cash reserves held by the fund.

Funds with betas greater than 1.0 during bull markets tend to have betas greater than 1.0 during bear markets. Some of the excess gains achieved during the bull-market phase may be wiped out during the bear-market phase. Similarly, those mutual funds with low betas during bull markets (i.e., below 1.0) tend to have low betas during bear markets. In theory, you can have a very volatile fund or a very stable fund, but differences in total returns are a function of the riskiness of a portfolio. The greater the risk, the greater the reward.

Funds with superior managers, however, may have betas that are higher during bull markets than they are during bear markets. For example, a fund might have a beta of 1.3 in a bull market and a beta of 1.0 in a bear market. Over time, that fund would rise much more rapidly in a bull market than the S&P 500 would. Over a complete market cycle, that fund theoretically would produce superior results.

Endnotes

1. Jill Bettner, "REIT Their Lips: Rating System Can Spot the Bargains," *The Wall Street Journal,* 21 December 1988, sec. c-1.
2. Based on a table from the *Hulbert Financial Digest,* 24 November 1987, and reprinted in "Who Saw It Coming and Who Didn't: Investment Advisers' Portfolios Before the Crash," *Barron's,* 7 December 1987.
3. Mark Hulbert, *Hulbert Financial Digest,* vol. XI, no. 5, 31 January 1991.
4. Others charge an exit fee at the time of the sale. This is another form of load fund.
5. Dr. Gary Zin, "Beat the Market with No-Load Funds," *Technical Analysis of Stocks and Commodities* (December 1989): 59–63.

2

Risk versus Reward

Professors of finance or economics used to argue that you cannot consistently beat the stock-market averages. Their articles often endorsed the random walk theory that says that there is no way to predict the future course of the stock market from current or past stock-market data. All the public information that could be known about a company already is contained in its price. Thus, technical analysis of stock prices cannot reveal anything not previously known. Supposedly, there is no way that you can pick stocks that will consistently outperform the rest of the market. The efficient market school insists that it is impossible to time the market, i.e., to anticipate major turning points in the stock market and to move in or out of stocks before the rest of the market can respond to the new trend.

PROBLEMS WITH THE EFFICIENT
MARKET HYPOTHESIS

The efficient market hypothesis presumes that the competition between analysts means that accurate and complete information is readily available to all investors. Many firms, however, concentrate the efforts of their analysts on the largest 1,000 companies (e.g., the Russell 1,000). Thus, literally thousands of smaller firms (e.g., the Russell 2,000) escape the regular scrutiny of the major analysts. When discussing the largest firms, the assumptions of the efficient market school seem appropriate. But when discussing the thousands of smaller firms ignored by analysts, those assumptions are less valid. To the extent that the small investor focuses his or her attention on smaller, local or regional companies, that person has an advantage over the large firms.

In addition, the early research of the efficient market school tended to be concerned rather narrowly with serial correlations in stock-market prices. Seldom did these studies ask whether an investment strategy based on technical analysis, sentiment, market valuation, interest-rate trends or economic data might improve total returns over time. Moreover, these authors seldom tested the models or timing systems actually employed by technical analysts. More recently, universities are tenuring and promoting people who are attacking the efficient market hypothesis that now has become a favorite whipping post of academicians.

TRADABLE EXCEPTIONS

Analysts have discovered a number of specific inefficiencies in the market. While that literature is too vast to be summarized here, six specific examples seem especially well documented and will serve to illustrate the point. First, just before each major holiday, the market tends to rise. Second, most of the gains in stock prices occur between the last three days of each month and the first six trading days of the next month. Third, during presidential-election years, the two months before the election usually see at least a 5 percent rally. Fourth, the two years following a presidential election usually witness a much weaker stock market than the two years immediately preceding a presidential election. Fifth, those who follow the (legal) insider-trading data can make additional profits by buying companies whose corporate officers are buying their own stock in large numbers. Sixth, most major market crashes occur at extremely high valuation levels, i.e., when price-earnings ratios and price-dividend ratios are excessively high. These patterns are based on extensive research and there are theoretical reasons why they occur. A full discussion of these reasons, however, is beyond the scope of the present effort. Perhaps one example might suffice.

The presidential-election effect is particularly interesting. Roger Huang argues that average gains in the first two years of a president's term are -2.57 percent versus +21.95 percent in the second two years.

An individual who invested in Treasury bills in the first two years and then held stocks in the second two years would have averaged 13.3 percent per year versus 8.2 percent per year for the buy-and-hold investor for the period 1961–1980.[1]

On the other hand, as investors become aware of these patterns, they may alter their behavior to take advantage of these opportunities. Thus, these tradable exceptions may disappear. For example, the so-called January effect is a tradable rally in the stock market beginning just after the conclusion of tax selling in mid-December. By the end of December or the beginning of January, investors begin to look for bargains among stocks that were sold off in December.

Quite often, over-the-counter (OTC) stocks do better than the Dow stocks during January. In 1988, however, investors jumped the gun on the summer rally, the presidential-election effect, tax selling and the January effect. Anticipation tends to flatten the gains made during such periods and moves their starting and ending dates ahead in time. In addition, in 1990, changes in tax laws forced mutual funds to sell stocks much earlier than normal and created a January effect in November!

ASSET-ALLOCATION FORMULAS

Most brokerages recommend asset-allocation strategies that adjust exposure to various markets based on the investor's general tolerance to risk or on current conditions in the marketplace. Even such famous random walkers as Burton Malkiel have suggested that allocations to stocks, bonds and cash be altered based on perceived risks and opportunities in the stock market. Many brokerage houses and national magazines advise investors to alter their asset mixture depending on whether they are conservative investors, moderately conservative or aggressive. Other analysts adjust exposure to the stock market because of an assessment of risk or opportunity in stocks, bonds, precious metals, real estate, etc.

Unfortunately, most people are likely to become more aggressive precisely at times when market risk is increasing, and they become less aggressive at times when market risk is extremely low. Investor psychology tends to be a lagging indicator, and, thus, it is dangerous for most people to adjust their exposure to risk based on generalized perceptions of market conditions.

Complex asset-allocation systems often include such things as U.S. bonds, U.S. stocks, cash, real estate, foreign bonds, foreign stocks and precious metals. These systems must be evaluated by modern portfolio theory to determine how well they really work. Unfortunately, that assessment is beyond the capabilities of most small investors. A long-term performance report going back five to ten years, however, should show you which systems have performed the best in good times and in bad. A much simpler and less expensive approach is an age-to-retirement formula along with stock-market timing for the equity portion of your assets. For many investors, that may represent an optimal balance between the need for safety and the desire for capital appreciation.

MARKET-TIMING THEORY

The efficient market hypothesis rejects stock-market timing. Many technical analysts, however, claim to have developed market-timing methods that will generate superior returns. Whether these work or not remains problematic. Research published by Jess Hua and Richard Woodward suggests that it is theoretically possible to beat the broader market averages through stock-market timing.[2] The authors claim, however, that it is more important to be able to identify bull markets than to identify bear markets. In theory, the buy-and-hold investor is 100 percent accurate in identifying bull markets and 0 percent accurate in identifying bear markets. The authors conclude that to be successful, you must be at least 70 percent successful in identifying both bull and bear markets or at least 80 percent successful in identifying bull markets and at least 50 percent successful in identifying bear markets.

EVIDENCE TO SUPPORT MARKET TIMING

Edward Renshaw developed a model for stock-market timing based on risk premiums, i.e., the difference between the yield on the S&P 500, the dividend-growth rate and the yield on Treasury bills.[3]

According to Renshaw, over 20 years, this timing method would have produced gains of 17.8 percent per year when the model flashed a buy signal and would have avoided losses of 6.1 percent per year when the model flashed a sell signal.

William Gray developed a similar model in 1978 using dividend growth and interest rates in his calculations.[4] He made projections based on his model for the S&P 400 Industrials, which then stood at 113. He called for the S&P 400 to triple by 15 October 1988. That would have required the S&P 400 to rise from 113 to 339 over ten years. By 24 October 1988, the S&P 400 reached an intraday high of 327.53 before selling off into the November lows. Thus, Gray's model had predicted a rise of 226 points over ten years, while the S&P 400 rose approximately 215 points. These results are extremely impressive.

Other scholars insist that you can beat the broader market averages through superior stock-picking strategies. Marc Reinganum, for example, has developed a system that produced annual returns of more than 30 percent per year, while the broader market rose only 5.9 percent per year.[5]

Thus, increasing evidence argues that the stock market is not perfectly efficient and that it is possible to beat the broader market averages. Market timing, however, takes a lot of time and effort—as well as some ability—to achieve excess returns.

Subsequent chapters will describe a variety of market-timing indicators. Each of these indicators has its strengths and weaknesses and must be used with caution. We will begin with macroeconomic indicators for these are so widely touted in the financial press. Most of this information is so quickly discounted by the financial markets, however, that most small investors are better advised to use macroeconomic indicators for general market orientation than for specific market timing.

A variety of technical indicators and simple market-timing models work reasonably well. Chapter 11 offers a series of six different models that are designed to provide the reader with alternative approaches to stock-market timing. The person who learns the strengths and weaknesses of these systems, who learns how to recognize when these models have given false signals and learns how to limit losses and let profits ride should do very well in the long run. But to use those models, you will have to gather some data and test them on your own. For the person who wants a simple, yet effective system, Chapter 12 offers my own market-timing model that is based on futures traders' sentiment.

PROFESSIONAL TIMING SERVICES

The number of macroeconomic indicators and timing systems built on these indicators is endless. Most individual investors have neither the time nor the training to develop their own market-timing models. A number of successful market-timing services, however, are available to the public. How good are they?

Evidence of the possibility of successful market timing comes from one of the most unlikely sources: Mark Hulbert. Hulbert is the editor of the *Hulbert Financial Digest*, a newsletter that rates the performance of investment advisory newsletters. Hulbert is regarded as a nuisance and gadfly by many advisers because he often points out how poorly their advice would have done when compared to a buy-and-hold strategy based on the ownership of a broadly diversified portfolio such as the stocks in the S&P 500. Hulbert reviewed the performance of 15 market timers that he follows in the May, 1989, issue of the *AAII Journal*.[6]

Hulbert concluded that "market timing's best foot is put forward when looked at on a risk-adjusted basis."[7] Hulbert's 15 timers offered a total of 30 different timing services. Nineteen beat the NYSE Composite Index on a risk-adjusted basis over the 50 months between January of 1985 and February of 1989. Eleven underperformed the market. The best service in this period was the "Elliott Wave Theorist (Investors)," with a risk-adjusted monthly return of 0.35 percent and a total return of 118.4 percent in 50 months versus a risk-adjusted return of 0.12 percent per month and a total return of 68.8 percent for the NYSE Composite Index (see Table 2.1). The worst of these 30 services had a return of -0.15 percent per month and a total return of -21.4 percent in 50 months. See Table 2.1 for those who produced at least a 0.24 percent risk-adjusted monthly return over that 50-month period. This record suggests that it may be possible to beat the broader

TABLE 2.1   Risk-Adjusted Newsletter Performance*

Newsletter	Risk-Adjusted	Total Return
Elliott Wave Theorist[1]	0.35%	118.4%
Lynn Elgert Report[2]	0.33	122.5
Lynn Elgert Report[3]	0.33	121.6
Stock Market Cycles[4]	0.33	109.9
Indicator Digest[5]	0.33	97.2
Mutual Fund Strategist[6]	0.24	88.5
Dow Theory Letters	0.24	87.7
NYSE	0.12	68.8

1. Investors
2. Long-term mutual fund switcher
3. Short-term mutual fund trader
4. Mutual fund switching advice
5. Short-term trading guide
6. Intermediate-term model
* Used with permission. See endnote 6.

market averages without taking on increased risk through leverage or the purchase of high beta stocks.

Another writer who tracks the performance of market timers is Steve Shellans, editor of the *MoniResearch Newsletter*. In 1990, Shellans described the recent performance of 17 professional market-timing services whose assets under management ranged from $2 million to $400 million.[8] Over a 12-month period ending 31 March 1990, the best of these services earned 24.7 percent (after dividends, interest and fees), while the worst earned 3.9 percent. While the S&P 500 earned 19.3 percent, including dividend reinvestment, the average of these 17 services earned only 13.8 percent. Thus, the record of the average market-timing service in that survey was unimpressive.

For the no-load mutual-fund investor, the most appropriate mar-ket- timing services might be those that issue only a few buy and sell signals each year, i.e., at the rate of one every two to three months. Such **intermediate-term** timing systems are reviewed regularly by *Timer Digest*. This publication follows some 90 professional timing services and ranks the top ten for the last 3, 6 and 12 months. In addition to *Timer Digest*, two alternative services review the performance of short-term timers. Harry Schiller's *Short-Term Timers Consensus Hotline* and Chip Hill's *Blue Chip Monitor* look at the performance of professional services that might generate more than one signal per day. To use such a service, you would have to be ready, willing and able to call several times per day for regular updates.

During the volatile period between 1 May 1990 and 31 October 1990, several of the timers followed by *Timer Digest* outperformed a buy-and-hold strategy. In fact, *Timer Digest*'s own Consensus Model beat the S&P 500 over three periods: 3, 6 and 12 months (ending 26 October 1990).

In any case, when you evaluate a market-timing system, look carefully at the capital appreciation earned by each system versus the capital appreciation of the S&P 500 over the same period. Because the period 1 January 1987 to 30 June 1991 was particularly difficult for market timers, a timing system's record over these four-and-a-half years should give you a much better idea of how well that method works in various types of markets. Be suspicious, however, if the timing service does not or will not furnish performance results for the entire period. Also be suspicious of theoretical results, i.e., models that are back-tested against historical data but that have not been traded in real time for several years over several different types of markets.

ROBERT NUROCK'S TECHNICAL MARKET INDEX

One example of an excellent professional timing system that meets these criteria is the original Technical Market Index (TMI) developed by Robert Nurock. John McGinley, the editor of *Technical Trends*, has said that the TMI is the "best single indicator" his service tracks for the period 6 to 12 months out.[9] While the TMI may not tell us what is likely to happen in the next few days and weeks, it does a good job of predicting significant market moves as far as six to nine months after the signal is given.

Unfortunately, a spat between Louis Rukeyser, the host of "Wall Street Week," and Robert Nurock, the creator of the TMI, led to Nurock's fall from grace. Thus, "Wall Street Week" no longer carries this indicator. Furthermore, Nurock has created a new TMI. Nevertheless, the original model serves as a good example of a sophisticated attempt at long-term stock-market timing.

The original TMI contained ten different technical indicators. It was particularly aimed at contrarians, i.e., those who prefer to take a **position** opposite that of the great majority of investors. In the past, the TMI was used to time major market changes using plus five as a buy signal and minus five as a sell signal.

Nurock's original model placed heavy emphasis on market action and investors' sentiment. Many of these indicators are widely followed by market technicians and test well against historical data. Nurock used a cumulative advance minus decline line, a new-highs minus new-lows index and three overbought/oversold indexes, including the Dow Jones momentum ratio, the Arms index and the prices of stocks on the NYSE versus their 10-week and 30-week moving averages. He also used the premium ratio on options, *Investor's Intelligence* surveys of advisory services, a low price-activity ratio, an insider-activity ratio and a ratio of the federal funds rate to the discount rate. The TMI is aimed at a long-term investor who does not want to spend a lot of time gathering and calculating technical data. In any case, if you decide to try to construct your own timing model, you would be well advised to look at the indicators that make up the TMI as your starting point.

Following the failure of the TMI to give a timely sell signal prior to the crash in 1987, Robert Nurock revised that system.[10] He also has developed a proprietary, short-term timing model, ESP, which has been made available through his newsletter, *Bob Nurock's Advisory*. This model may be more appropriate for a more aggressive investor willing to trade every few months.

MARTIN ZWEIG'S SUPER MODEL

In his book, *Winning on Wall Street,* Martin Zweig developed a Super Model that uses a limited number of monetary and market indicators to generate buy and sell signals. These appear to provide generally good signals for both intermediate-term and long-term investors and would seem to outperform a buy-and-hold approach. The model only generates one to two round-trip signals per year and, thus, is compatible with most mutual funds switching limitations. From

1970 to 1987, it generated 17 buy and sell signals. Following this system requires that an investor spend perhaps 15 to 20 minutes per week gathering data from *Barron's* and entering it in a worksheet. Unfortunately, the complicated system of model points may inhibit its adoption by most people.

Among his four major components, Zweig looks at the prime rate. Zweig says that a rise in the prime rate is negative and a decline in the prime rate is positive for stocks. He admits that the prime rate lags behind other interest rates but argues that there is a lag between changes in Federal Reserve policy and changes in the stock market. The lag between the prime rate and Federal Reserve policy makes it possible to enter or exit the market closer to actual turning points. See Zweig's book, *Winning on Wall Street,* for further details on calculating indicator points from the prime rate.

Second, Zweig uses changes in the discount rate to generate additional signals. Again, the discount rate is a lagging indicator of other interest rates. Because the discount rate lags behind other rates, it reflects recent changes in Federal Reserve policy and not the start of a new direction in Federal Reserve policy. The psychological impact of a hike (or decline) in the discount rate on the financial markets, however, can be dramatic because many observers remain skeptical in the face of rising (or falling) interest rates until some official public action removes all shadow of a doubt.

Third, Zweig compares nonseasonally adjusted consumer installment debt for any one month to the same month during the previous year, e.g., June of 1988 to June of 1987. (An alternative to consumer installment debt might be the consumer-debt/income ratio. This ratio has the advantage of focusing directly on the degree to which consumers remain relatively liquid.)[11] Presumably, the more the average individual is heavily in debt, the less likely he or she is to invest additional capital in stocks.

The recent popularity of home-equity loans may have distorted this indicator somewhat. New tax laws permit deduction of the interest paid only on home-equity loans. As a result, some consumers have shifted part of their debt burden from consumer installment debt to home-equity loans. Thus, a combination of consumer installment debt and home-equity loans probably will give more accurate signals in the future.

Consumer-installment-debt statistics are released about six to eight weeks late. So, you tend to be using this month's interest rate and market data with consumer-debt information that is one to two months old. How this affects Zweig's model is uncertain.

Fourth, Zweig uses the *Value Line* Composite Index to calculate additional buy and sell signals. The *Value Line* index contains 1,700 stocks and thus represents the broader market. Unfortunately, institutions have tended to dominate equity markets during the 1980s. This has led to emphasis on trading stocks in companies with high daily volume. Thus, blue chip stocks have flourished, while smaller capitalization stocks have languished. How this will affect Zweig's model in the future also is uncertain.

Finally, Zweig puts all four indicators together into a Super Model based on a complicated system of model points. Unfortunately, many investors may find it difficult to calculate the various indicator and model points. Even the best model will provide mediocre results if you do not follow it faithfully.

DO IT YOURSELF?

For those who would seek to develop their own timing models, the problem is quite challenging. Many long-term timing models generate buy and sell signals weeks or months before the actual top (or bottom) is reached. If you follow these models, you will be out of the market while others are fully invested and in stocks while others are on the sidelines. You must be disciplined in your approach to investing and have the courage of your convictions. It may prove hard to keep up your confidence in the face of a plethora of contradictory advice that can create all kinds of second thoughts. On the other hand, the creation of market-timing models is the one area of technical analysis that seems to hold out the prospect of superior returns for someone engaged in other, full-time professional activity.

A PRACTICAL EXAMPLE:
BLUE CHIPS VERSUS SECONDARY ISSUES

One of the simplest yet most promising long-term, market-timing systems is really an allocation system that indicates when you should be investing in high-capitalization stocks or in low-capitalization stocks, i.e., in the stocks of very large and well-established companies with excellent balance sheets and relatively established markets or in the stocks of high-growth companies that are relatively small in size and still competing for a larger market share, often in a new industry.

Although secondary issues (growth stocks) often outperform the DJIA, at times, high-capitalization stocks outperform secondary issues. A rough rule of thumb, however, can be applied to determine when the secondary issues are overpriced or underpriced as a group. Using T. Rowe Price's New Horizons fund as a surrogate for the secondary issues, when the P/E ratio of this fund drops to the level of the S&P 500, i.e., a ratio of one to one, then secondary issues are grossly underpriced. When the P/E ratio is double that of the broader market (a ratio of two to one), secondary issues are overpriced.[12]

You might develop an asset-allocation strategy in which you would allocate 100 percent of your money to a blue chip mutual fund when the ratio reached 2.00 to 1; 75 percent when it reached 1.75 to 1; 50 percent when it reached 1.50 to 1; 25 percent when it reached 1.25 to 1; and 0 percent when it reached 1.00 to 1. Between these benchmarks, subtract 1.00 from the ratio and use the remainder as your percentage to invest in blue chip stocks. (The rest of your funds would be invested in a small-capitalization mutual fund that tracks the NASDAQ or the Russell 2,000.) Such a rule could direct your investments profitably from one type of indexed fund to another—adding to the return to any fund market-timing system. This simple system is one of the more promising ways for the average investor to try to beat the broader market averages.

Endnotes

1. See Roger D. Huang, "Common Stock Returns and Presidential Elections," *Financial Analysts Journal* (March–April 1985): 58–61.

2. Jess C. Hua and Richard S. Woodward, *Gains From Stock Market Timing,* Monograph Series in Finance and Economics, Salomon Brothers Center for the Study of Financial Institutions, Graduate School of Business Administration, New York University, 1986, 14–15.

3. Edward Renshaw, *Journal of Portfolio Management* (Summer 1985): 33–35.

4. William S. Gray, *Journal of Portfolio Management* (Summer 1984): 73–80.

5. Marc R. Reinganum, "The Anatomy of a Stock Market Winner," *Financial Analysts Journal* (March–April, 1988): 16–28.

6. Mark Hulbert, "To Time or Not To Time: A Look at More Evidence," *AAII Journal,* vol. 11, no. 5 (May 1989): 22–24. Reprinted with permission. © 1989 *Hulbert Financial Digest,* 316 Commerce St., Alexandria, VA 22314. Also reprinted with the permission of the American Association of Individual Investors, 625 N. Michigan Ave., Chicago, IL 60611.

7. Ibid., p. 23.

8. *MoniResearch Newsletter,* vol. 5, no. 2 (May–June 1990): 2.

9. Interview with John Bollinger on FNN, 14 February 1989.

10. The revised TMI was described on FNN's Wednesday half-hour edition of "Shop Talk" during an interview with Jeff Bower on 10 October 1990. Descriptions of his indicators and charts of their performance since 1978 can be obtained from the author, c/o *Bob Nurock's Advisory,* P. O. Box 988, Paoli, PA 19301.

11. Suggested by Maury Harris of PaineWebber in an interview on FNN with Ron Insana, 12 December 1988.

12. James Collins, ed., *OTC Insight,* in an interview on FNN with Bill Griffeth on "Market Wrap," 22 November 1988.

3

Business Cycles and the Stock Market

A number of analysts study macroeconomic data to try to predict the course of the stock market. Some of their models are quite sophisticated and lie well beyond the capabilities of the average investor armed only with a desktop PC. Fortunately, however, several fairly simple ways are available to gain some sense of the general health of the stock market based on data readily obtainable from such sources as *The Wall Street Journal* and *Barron's*, e.g., corporate profits, reported earnings, retail sales, automobile sales, new housing construction, construction permits, unemployment, new jobs creation, purchasing managers' reports, the Producer Price Index (PPI), the Consumer Price Index (CPI), the fixed weight deflator, the trade surplus (deficit), the gross national product (GNP), etc.

It is extremely important to adjust macroeconomic indicators for inflation. While most analysts simply look at the trend in the crude data, an adjustment for the cost of living provides a much better indication of the real direction of the economy

BUSINESS-CYCLE MODEL

To get some sense of the health of the economy and the level of risk in the market, you might begin your analysis with a look at Martin Pring's business-cycle model.[1] Pring believes that stock-market prices are closely tied to both the business cycle and interest rates. Pring regards rising bond prices as marking the start of a recession at Stage One of the business cycle. Stage Two begins as stock prices rise and the recession bottoms out. Stage Three starts as the recovery continues and commodity prices begin to rise. Bond prices, however, begin to decline at the very end of Stage Three. Stage Four starts as the recovery is moving ahead strongly. Stage Five witnesses declining stock and bond prices and rising commodity prices. Stage Six begins with declining commodity prices as the economy already has begun to turn down from its peak. Supposedly, you want to buy stocks at the beginning of Stage Two and sell them at the beginning of Stage Five.

Next, look at James McWilliams's model that provides a method of estimating the current position within the business cycle.[2] McWilliams associates the maximum rate of M2 growth, a peak in labor productivity, sharply rising housing starts and low inflation with 9:00 A.M.; sharp increases in the prime rate, corporate capital expansion and improvement projects started, commercial paper volume up and reports of poor vendor performance with 11:00 A.M., the selling opportunity; shrinkage of real money supply, sharp rises in short-term interest rates, soaring inflation and sharp increases in overtime with the peak of the boom, i.e., 12:00 P.M.; declining short-term interest rates, easier monetary policy, new orders falling off and at least six months since the peak in the stock market with 3:00 P.M.; an increase in money supply, market yields above 3.7 percent, P/E ratios below 14 times, construction at a low point and consumer confidence falling with 4:00 P.M.; and the rate of change of real M2 growth changing from negative to positive, high levels of bankruptcies, union emphasis on job security issues and pessimism in the popular press with 5:00 P.M., the buying opportunity.

EARLY WARNING SIGNS

Most small investors are attracted to the market at times when the economy is booming and the stock market is making a series of new, all-time highs. Yet, such times may be fraught with danger. Several indicators provide early warning signals of the end of a period of expansion. Usually, these signals precede the end of a bull market. One is a decline in new housing starts. This indicator is particularly sensitive to easy- and tight-money conditions. Wilfred R. George suggested using a figure of 1.5 million new starts per month as a buy or sell signal. As new housing starts fall below 1.5 million, sell stocks. As they climb above 1.5 million, buy stocks. The problem with using 1.5 million units is that new housing starts are strongly influenced by the rate of family formation. It might be better to take a long-term moving average (e.g., 12 months) and compare the current level to that average and devise a more appropriate index.

Another interest-rate sensitive indicator often associated with the end of the business cycle is automobile sales. Automobile manufacturers often provide low-interest financing as well as special incentives such as rebates. Thus, monthly automobile sales can be somewhat unreliable as an indicator, although declines in seasonally adjusted automobile sales over two to three months should be taken as a possible sign of the end of the business cycle.

Other indicators include a decline in the rate of growth of business investment, a decline in the growth of real money supply, a decline in the growth of real consumer spending and changes in base metal prices. According to some analysts, copper prices often spike toward the very end of the business cycle. Because steel stocks tend to rise toward the latter stages of an economic expansion, when those stocks start to show poor chart patterns after a long rally, the end of an economic cycle may be near.

The list of possible indicators is endless. Delos Smith, an economist with the Conference Board, however, has identified ten indicators that suggest an overheating economy often associated with the end of both a business and a stock-market cycle.[3] These include the length of the workweek, the level of backlogs, capacity utilization, wage increases, the unemployment rate, productivity weakness, accelerating unit labor costs, rising interest rates, uneasy financial markets and tight markets for labor and facilities. Smith suggested that 85 percent is sometimes regarded as the moral equivalent of full capacity. In regard to unemployment, he said that anything below 5.5 percent was a warning sign.

In 1989, a decline in housing starts, followed by a decline in automobile sales, seemed to coincide with a change in the real growth of M2 from positive to negative. In addition, copper prices had spiked and then began to decline. Also, Treasury-bill rates spiked above their long-term up-channel. Finally, there were alarming spikes in the PPI and the CPI in the first quarter of 1989. By the second half of 1989, the broader market began to turn down sharply, despite a rise in blue chip stocks. This points out the danger in focusing exclusively on large capitalization stocks to test macroeconomic timing models. Macroeconomic indicators may work better for the Russell 2,000 than for the Dow Jones Industrial Average (DJIA).

At the end of a recession, a rise in new housing permits and new housing starts often is the first encouraging sign. A slowing in the rate of increase of new jobless claims also will anticipate the bottom of the recession. Declining inflation, increases in the money supply and lower real, short-term interest rates also are encouraging signs.

LEADING ECONOMIC INDICATORS

The Leading Economic Indicators (LEIs), which were revised in 1989, supposedly predict the future strength of the economy some six months ahead. This data, however, is subject to substantial revision over the next several months that may considerably shorten the forecasting window (i.e., the amount of lead time) provided by the LEIs. Generally, economists regard three declines in a row in the LEIs as indicating the possibility of a recession within the next six months or so.

The LEIs are useful but should be employed with some caution. In fact, a subset of the LEIs may be more useful than the entire index. According to Martin Pring, Columbia University's index of long leading indicators is useful to anticipate changes in the stock market. Others have suggested using the ratio of lagging indicators to coincident indicators.

One system that seems particularly straightforward was suggested by Jim Benham. Benham recommends that you look at the **year-over-year** change in the LEIs to signal a possible recession or recovery.[4] Benham says that a possible recession is signaled when the year-over-year change drops below zero and a recovery is indicated when that change rises above zero. Thus, the LEIs help the investor to develop a clearer impression of the prospects for the economy over the next several months.

MONEY SUPPLY

The relationship between money supply and the economy is a source of enormous debate between the monetarist school and the neo-Keynesian school. Similarly, the usefulness of monetary data in stock-market timing remains controversial. In an era of global markets and international money flows, it is potentially quite misleading to look at the monetary data for just one country. The issues are so complex, however, that they should be discussed within the context of American monetary policy first and then international monetary policy second.

Economists disagree sharply over the time lag between changes in the money supply and changes in stock prices. Some experts have claimed that a change in money supply is felt by the markets four to eight weeks later. Others claim that the interval is as long as 9 to 15 months.

How do we reconcile these conflicting claims? A decline in the growth rate of real money supply usually precedes a decline in stock prices by 9 to 11 months and a downturn in the business cycle by 15 to 16 months.[5] This opinion is shared by a variety of analysts including John Bollinger, who uses a six-month rate of change in M3 as an indicator.[6] Bollinger says that a change in this indicator usually precedes changes in the stock market by 6 to 12 months.

An increase in the real growth rate of money supply usually precedes an upturn in stock prices by three to four months and an improvement in business conditions by an average of eight months. These averages, however, are subject to wide variation and offer approximate rather than specific targets.

In 1988, the growth rate of M2 increased from 3.4 percent in January to 4.3 percent in February to 4.75 percent in March to 5.08 percent in April to 5.5 percent in May. At the end of May, after four months of increasing growth in M2, the market rallied sharply. Someone following this indicator would have invested at about 1,941 on the Dow and had a gain of 200+ points—or more than 10 percent in one month.

Once again, in September of 1990, the real money supply growth rate had been around -4 percent until the Federal Reserve System began increasing bank reserves and lowering the discount rate starting in October. By January of 1991, the stock market began a sharp rally that eventually carried it to all-time new highs. Then, real money supply growth stabilized around -2 percent in February of 1991 and the stock market entered a broad trading range between 2,850 on the downside and 3,000 on the upside. Was this a coincidence? Hardly.

Measure monetary growth by the **year-to-date** rate of change, after adjusting for changes in the CPI. The easiest way to do this is to divide the M1, M2, M3, M4 or "L" figure for the current month by the data for the same month the year before.

(Current M2 ÷ Year-ago M2) ÷ (Current CPI ÷ Year-ago CPI)

Then, divide this ratio by the current CPI data divided by the CPI for the previous 12 months. (This creates a ratio of a ratio.) When this ratio is increasing, conditions are positive for the stock market. When this ratio is decreasing, conditions are turning negative for the stock market. When the ratio declines from above 1.0 to below 1.0, a sell signal is given. When the ratio rises from below 1.0 to above 1.0, a buy signal is generated.

This is not, by itself, a very useful short-term market-timing tool for investors simply do not understand the lag between changes in money supply growth and changes in economic activity. This ratio of ratios is useful, however, because it points out times in which monetary conditions are generally favorable or unfavorable for the long run.

Ned Davis uses a ten-month moving average of real M2 growth versus the monthly data. He says that "when real money supply goes below its ten-month moving average, that's a sell signal, and when it goes above, that's a buy signal." Davis claims that a positive signal is associated with a 9.2 percent annual gain in market values versus a 4.5 percent loss in market values after a sell signal. He also claims that 92 percent of all signals have been profitable since 1960.

Davis also looks at real M3 versus real GNP. When real M3 drops below zero growth and below real GNP, a warning of a major bear market is given. In fact, Davis's associate, Craig Corcoran, has claimed that negative real growth of M3 always has indicated a hard landing for the economy. Corcoran looks at the differential between the year-to-year growth rate of real M3 and the year-to-year growth rate of real

GNP to forecast how bad a recession might be after real year-to-year M3 growth drops below zero.

In late 1990, Jim Benham suggested that the optimists who were looking for a quick recovery from the 1990-1991 recession might be disappointed because the year-over-year growth in real M2 still was negative. Benham argued that there is about a nine-month lag between real M2 turning positive and the start of economic recovery.

FEDERAL RESERVE SYSTEM AND
INTEREST RATES

One of the most popular forms of macroeconomic analysis is the study of Federal Reserve policy regarding interest rates. Many investors are convinced that a steady rise in interest rates generally is negative for the economy and stock market, while a steady decline in interest rates generally is quite good for the economy and the stock market. (Real interest rates are far more important than nominal interest rates, but that will be discussed in Chapter 4.) The fact that so many people possess these beliefs creates a form of self-fulfilling prophecy. Thus, a study of Federal Reserve policy is a fruitful area of investigation for the market timer.

Because the Federal Reserve System is charged with trying to stabilize the economy and fight inflation, the Fed often tightens monetary policy in the face of a potentially inflationary expansion and loosens monetary policy in the face of looming recessions.

DISCOUNT RATE

While analysts agree that the tightening or loosening of monetary policy by the Federal Reserve System affects both the economy and the stock market, there is considerable disagreement on the importance of the **discount rate**. Some analysts regard it as a lagging indicator, while others believe that changes in the discount rate can have an important **announcement effect** on the stock market. In fact, the discount rate is a lagging rate with more psychological significance than direct economic impact. Discount rate changes are strong signals from the Fed regarding their perception of the economy. As such, they tend to convince the myriad doubting Thomases and lead to a major swing in residual sentiment in favor of a higher (or lower) interest-rate scenario.

Two different but related rules attributed to Edson Gould and Norman Fosback, respectively, summarize the extant wisdom of the analysts. Three steps and a stumble refers to a predicted drop in stock-market prices after the Federal Reserve has tightened monetary policy by three successive increases in the discount rate. Two drops and a jump refers to a predicted rise in the stock market after two successive decreases in the discount rate. These rules reflect the belief that attempts by the Fed to ease monetary policy stimulate a weak economy more profoundly than attempts to tighten monetary policy restrain a booming economy.

Unfortunately, research suggests that these rules do not always work the way analysts expect. Arthur Bonnel has studied Gould's three steps and a stumble rule in detail.[7] He argues that enormous fluctuations in the market's performance occur after the sell signal is triggered. Bonnel studied the ten signals since 1919 and found an average rise in the stock market of 15.6 percent in the 8.4 months immediately following a sell signal, followed by an average decline of 27.7 percent over a total of 24.5 months. Thus, after about nine months, the market should begin a slide of approximately 32 percent from its ultimate high—in theory. Despite its limitations, the discount rate still has a powerful effect on the stock market, and investors who ignore changes in that rate do so at their own risk!

FED WATCHING

You can watch for signs of possible changes in Federal Reserve policy by watching system repurchases and matched sales. A repurchase occurs when the Federal Reserve System buys back Treasury securities previously sold to member banks. This increases the cash held by member banks and thus helps to increase the money supply as well as to reduce the federal funds rate.

A system repurchase (which injects liquidity into the banking system) indicates a stronger move than a customer repurchase. Also, an overnight repurchase carries a stronger message, i.e., it conveys a sense of greater urgency, than does a normal repurchase.

If, for example, the federal funds rate is rising and the Fed wishes to check that rise, it will repurchase securities, injecting more funds into the system. If the federal funds rate is declining, however, and the Fed wants to stop that decline, it will sell securities to member banks, thus reducing ready cash and increasing the federal funds rate or checking its decline.

If the Fed allows the federal funds rate to rise (or decline) without intervening at the market at the normal time, this can be considered a confirmation of the new trend. CNBC/FNN often carries updates that indicate whether or not the Fed has intervened in the capital markets.

FEDERAL FUNDS RATE

There are many experts whose wishful thinking interferes with their analyses. Most people would be much better off to chart the actual level of the federal funds rate over time than to try to guess what the Fed should be doing or to listen to various self-appointed Fed watchers. Three notable exceptions to this rule, however, are Ed Hart, Jim Benham and David Jones.

As the upper half of Figure 3.1 indicates, the federal funds rate rose from approximately 6.0 percent in July 1987 to 7.5 percent by October of 1987, a relative increase of 25 percent. Those who followed a chart of the federal funds rate should have grown progressively more cautious as stock prices reached all-time highs in terms of price-earnings, price-dividend and price-to-book ratios while the federal funds rate was rising so rapidly.

INFLATION

High rates of inflation hurt corporate earnings and encourage investors to turn to precious metals, real estate or cash equivalents to protect purchasing power. Therefore, inflation tends to depress stock prices. As a result, the anticipation of high rates of inflation will lead investors into precious metals and natural resources and away from

FIGURE 3.1   Federal Funds Rate, March–December 1987

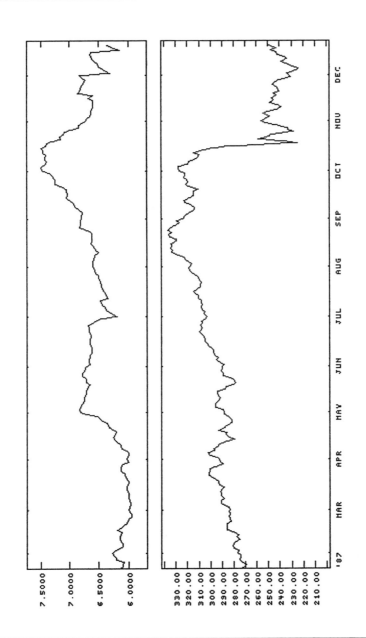

stocks and bonds, just as the anticipation of low rates of inflation will lead investors into stocks and bonds and out of cash and precious metals.

Many analysts use the gold index as an estimate of future inflation. This may not be wise. Gold prices may be better regarded as a coincident indicator of the expectation of inflation in the future. Because gold prices are affected by supply and demand factors as well as by changes in the value of the dollar, fluctuations in the price of gold sometimes may be more related to the supply of gold on world markets and to changes in the value of the dollar than to changing expectations of inflation.

Although declining inflation (disinflation) generally is regarded as positive for stocks, price decline (deflation) is characteristic of recessions and depressions and thus not associated with a strong stock market. What you need is low or declining inflation coupled with good prospects for the economy.

CONSUMER PRICE INDEX (CPI)

Many analysts focus on the Consumer Price Index (CPI) as a guide to inflation. If the CPI is increasing rapidly, then fears of inflation tend to be widespread and strong. If the CPI is flat or declining, then fears of inflation probably are low. Larry Kimball, an economist at UCLA, suggests using a three-month or even a six-month moving average of the CPI to measure inflation.[8] This makes sense because most analysts tend to discount one or even two months of aberrant data. In addition, the underlying series, especially for food and energy, are so volatile that many analysts prefer to see a trend in place for several months before they are confident that the rate of inflation has changed on a permanent basis rather than experienced a temporary fluctuation.

When earnings growth is strong and inflation is weak, the stock-market outlook is quite bullish. By contrast, when earnings growth is weak and inflation (as measured by the CPI) is strong, the outlook for the stock market is quite bearish. This is, perhaps, one of the great lessons of the postcrash environment of 1988–1989. Another is that most brokers and fund managers use P/E ratios in a simplistic way and thus their decisions tend to be very strongly influenced by market, industry and firm P/Es, regardless of inflation, price-dividend ratios or price-to-book ratios.

The investing public is slow to change its outlook on inflation and depends heavily on the CPI, despite its limitations. To gain an advantage on the investing public, you need an indicator that might give you a warning of future changes in the CPI. Fortunately, several indicators might prove useful.

PRODUCER PRICE INDEX (PPI)

The Producer Price Index (PPI) for finished goods occasionally provides a warning of future increases in the CPI. It also is widely followed by Wall Street analysts. The forecasting window provided by that indicator, however, is inconsistent. At times, the PPI for finished goods is a leading indicator; at other times, it is a coincident indicator. Ned Davis uses the PPI to generate sell signals for the stock market.[9] According to Davis, to get a sell signal, the PPI has to rise 4 percent from the low in the cycle. He says that 14 out of 16 signals have been profitable since 1965 and you would have made 11.6 percent per annum versus 3.9 percent on a buy-and-hold basis.

The PPIs for crude goods and intermediate goods might prove more useful as indicators of future inflation than the PPI for finished goods. This is because crude and intermediate goods reflect the impact of inflation or deflation earlier in the cycle than do finished goods. (Similarly, base metals, such as copper, lead, zinc and aluminum, often reflect inflationary pressures sooner than gold and silver.) Data for the PPI can be found in issues of the *Value Line Investment Survey*, available at most public libraries.

PURCHASING MANAGERS INDEX

Among the more useful and widely followed monthly statistics is the National Association of Purchasing Managers (NAPM) index that indicates the number of purchasing managers who see their businesses expanding. Any figure greater than 50 percent indicates a growing economy. The trend in these statistics is extremely useful. Some experts suggest that three reports in a row below 50 percent predict a future recession, much as three monthly declines in a row in the LEIs predict a recession. In addition, some analysts claim that any monthly reading below 44 percent suggests that the nation is already in a recession. This index seems to be a much more stable indicator of the direction of the industrial economy than is the LEI and much less subject to gut-wrenching revisions.

Another popular variant on this system is the Chicago-based purchasing managers report that comes out a day ahead of the national survey. It is not seasonally adjusted, however, and therefore is less useful than the NAPM report.

COMMODITIES RESEARCH BUREAU (CRB)

Many analysts look at the Commodities Research Bureau (CRB) index of 21 commodities for signs of possible inflation or deflation. The CRB, however, is heavily weighted toward grains, while oil is underweighted. Thus, some analysts think the CRB is not a particularly reliable indicator of changes in the CPI, while others place great emphasis on that index. Because the CRB seems closely related to bond prices (a rising CRB is negative for bonds, while a declining CRB is positive for bonds), a wise bond investor watches the CRB closely. Furthermore, because rising bond prices usually are positive for the stock market, sophisticated equity traders also watch the CRB.

BANK CREDIT AND DEBIT DATA

Bank credit and debit information may provide some indication of long-term economic vitality. Unfortunately, such data is very hard to find on a timely basis and the average investor must look at Federal Reserve publications for that information.

A. Hamilton Bolton believed in a 15-year credit cycle. He suggested that total bank debits are very strongly correlated with national income and the GNP. Changes in bank debits over time are a good measure of the expansion (or contraction) of economic activity. In fact,

Bolton insisted that bank debits are a more timely and accurate indicator of total economic activity than the GNP alone.

LOAN-CREDIT RATIO

Another very useful measure is the loan-credit ratio that reveals the ease with which the Federal Reserve System can expand or contract the money supply and the total debt as well. The higher the ratio, the more impact Fed policies can have in contracting outstanding loans. The lower the ratio, the less impact the Fed can have in contracting loans. Furthermore, at low loan-credit ratios, the Fed cannot guarantee that further increases in the money supply will not result in reductions of velocity.

NET-FREE (BORROWED) RESERVES

The Federal Reserve System has greater control over bank reserves than it does over interest rates or the money supply, per se. Some analysts claim that the Fed's intentions are best understood through a close reading of changes in net reserves. A three-week moving average of bank net-free reserves is a useful indicator of current liquidity trends. Presumably, changes in free reserves tended to be reflected in the stock market approximately one month later.[10] Fortunately, such data is readily found in both *Barron's* and *The Wall Street Journal*.

NEED FOR CAUTION

The analysis of business cycles and macroeconomic data can be very useful if you want to develop a long-term outlook for the stock market. Economic data, however, often are subject to substantial revisions long after they have been released. Thus, to act on the release of new government statistics is very dangerous. Moreover, professional economists argue constantly about the meaning of these statistics. How can an average investor make sense out of fragmentary and often erroneous data when the professionals disagree so violently?

Most technical analysts concentrate their attention on the stock market itself to generate actual buy and sell signals. It is not that macroeconomic data are unimportant. It is simply that the relationship between that data and the markets is complex. Also, the time lag between changes in macroeconomic data and the response of the market is highly variable.

In some cases, the stock market may correctly anticipate the release of unemployment, housing or inflation data. If so, the market may have fully discounted that information and might not react at all when the official statistics are released. At other times, analysts' expectations prove to be far off the mark and the stock market may react violently to the official release. Because macroeconomic data are subject to wide revisions after they are released, any decisions based on the original statistics may be invalidated. In any case, because the markets discount information so quickly, the private investor who does not follow the markets full-time has little chance of gaining an advantage over professional investors who study the same data.

Endnotes

1. Described in Pring's *Interest Rate Review*, vol. 1 no. 1 (March 1989): 10–11.
2. James D. McWilliams, "Watchman tell us of the night!", *Journal of Portfolio Management* (Spring 1984): 75–88.
3. "Market Wrap," interview with Bill Griffeth, FNN, 18 August 1988.
4. "Market Wrap," interview with Bill Griffeth, FNN, 29 June 1989.
5. Wilfred R. George, *Tight Money Timing* (New York: Praeger, 1982), p. 68.
6. "Shop Talk," FNN, 6 February 1990.
7. "Market Wrap," interview with Bill Griffeth, FNN, 15 March 1989.
8. "Shop Talk," FNN, 18 May 1989.
9. *Barron's*, 27 March 1989.
10. James Welsh, "The Financial Commentator," "Market Wrap," interview with Bill Griffeth, FNN, 22 September 1988.

4

Buy Low—Sell High: Is the Market Cheap or Expensive?

Macroeconomic indicators tell the investor where the economy might be headed over the weeks and months ahead. The relationship between the economy and the stock market, however, is extraordinarily complex. Even if the outlook for the economy is poor but stocks are cheap, sophisticated investors will start accumulating stocks. On the other hand, if the outlook for the economy is positive but stocks are expensive, wise investors will begin to sell stocks.

To buy low and sell high is the hope of every investor. But exactly how do you judge when to sell? And how do experienced investors determine whether the market is really cheap or expensive? This chapter examines several traditional measures of market value and offers an eclectic approach that avoids the pitfall of depending on any one indicator, no matter how popular.

DIVIDEND YIELDS

One popular market-timing system is based on dividend yields. Experience suggests that yields on stocks rarely exceed 6 percent. At that level, stocks have tended to rally strongly for several months or even years. The prospects for long-term capital gains are excellent. Similarly, when yields are below 3 percent, the chances of a major decline in stock prices increase dramatically. Hindsight suggests that someone who invested in stocks only when yields were greater than 6 percent and held those stocks until yields dropped below 3 percent would have a total return of 17 percent compounded annually versus 9 percent for the buy-and-hold investor.[1]

Few investors, however, are likely to find such a system satisfactory because you would be out of the market for extremely long periods of time while others were making huge gains on their investments. There would be a strong tendency to abandon the system and get in on the action. This system also would require you to buy stocks when the financial news was the gloomiest and sell stocks when the news was filled with excellent reports on the economy. Most people would find that very hard to do. Thus, this particular system may not be practical. It is a useful example, however, of a basic valuation approach that could increase total returns over a buy-and-hold strategy. It also suggests that there are times when the individual investor must be extremely conservative and other times when it pays to be a bit more aggressive.[2]

At the very least, the dividend yield gives you some sense of whether you should be generally optimistic or pessimistic about the market's prospects. In your analysis, use yields on indexes such as the S&P 500 or the NYSE rather than the DJIA. The DJIA contains only 30 stocks, and thus an exceptional situation for one company can have a major effect on the average.[3]

PRICE-DIVIDEND RATIO

An important and extremely useful variation on dividend yields is the **price-dividend ratio**. Craig Corcoran points out that the 62-year average for the price-dividend ratio has been 24. According to Richard Russell, the Dow has reached the 30-to-1 price-dividend ratio on 17 occasions since 1971.[4] On average, the market has declined 36 percent after it peaked out. As a result, a number of professional investment advisers begin to get anxious as price-dividend ratios climb above 30. Similarly, when the price-dividend ratio drops below 20 to 1, the market is often regarded as very inexpensive.

There are some limitations to timing systems based on either price-dividend ratios or dividend yields. Dividend growth is slow. Companies tend to be very conservative in raising dividends and very, very reluctant to lower them. During periods of very rapid growth in net corporate profits (earnings), dividends tend to grow slowly. Dividend growth may tend to increase toward the end of long periods of expansion, resulting in declining price-dividend ratios, not increasing ratios, at market tops. Moreover, a rising payout ratio (the percentage of corporate earnings paid to stockholders as dividends) may conceal what is really happening. For example, in 1989, rising dividends were the result of increases in the payout ratio, masking declines in corporate operating profits.

The payout ratio may fluctuate for other reasons. For example, new management may decide to retain a greater percentage of increasing earnings to plow back into research and development or pay off corporate debts. Meanwhile, dividends may remain constant. Under these circumstances, a declining payout ratio does not reflect corporate uncertainty about the future trend of corporate profits, but rather a reorientation of the company toward higher rates of growth.

Despite these caveats, the price-dividend ratio ought to be regarded as a very useful guide to the level of market values. But it should not be used as an isolated market-timing tool. A basket of value indicators can provide some protection against misinterpretation of any single indicator. For the average investor who often is unaware of accounting gimmickry, this collective approach to market valuation seems particularly appropriate.

BOOK VALUE

Book value is another popular measure of a company's net worth. It is the difference between assets and liabilities. Unfortunately, there are significant problems with this indicator that prevent it from being used with complete confidence. Assets that have been held for a long time by a company may be listed at their purchase price, not their replacement value. Thus, on a book-value basis, a company's stock might look quite expensive but a look at the replacement costs of assets might suggest something quite different. Nevertheless, book value can be a useful, if crude indicator of whether the stock market is relatively overvalued or undervalued. For example, from 1942 to 1988, the price-to-book ratio ranged from a high of 2.76 to a low of 0.80[5] with an annual average of 1.64 for the high and 1.32 for the low.[6] The problem with these historical benchmarks is that the financial system became excessively **leveraged** in the 1980s and what was previously considered a very high **price-to-book ratio** is now considered more normal. Whether the experience of the 1990s proves that recent valuations are dangerously high remains to be seen.

PRICE-EARNINGS RATIO

Perhaps the most widely followed market valuation indicator is the **price-earnings ratio** (P/E) for the overall market. Investment advisers and technical analysts love to quote the P/E and become quite bullish when the market's P/E is low and become quite bearish when it is high. The average investor, however, is very likely to get confused when some analysts are saying that market's P/E is normal while other analysts claim that it is expensive.

A market P/E of 20 to 1 suggests an expensive market, while a P/E of 10 to 1 suggests a cheap market. Unfortunately, changes in tax laws, accounting procedures and inventory control (e.g., just-in-time manufacturing) can cause tremendous changes in P/E ratios—without any real changes in reported earnings.[7] In 1989, many brokers and analysts kept claiming that the stock market was relatively cheap based on the overall P/E ratio, while other methods of valuation suggested that the market was getting quite expensive. This was extremely confusing to most average investors. Who was right?

In 1986, new tax laws allowed companies to take accelerated depreciation. This reduced corporate earnings in the short run and then led to sharp increases in reported corporate earnings in 1987–1989. At the same time, corporate operating profits had changed very little. In short, the impact of changes in the tax codes affected corporate earnings far more than dividends or book value.

To judge for yourself whether the market is relatively cheap or expensive, look at three indicators: the price-dividend ratio, the price-to-book ratio and the price-earnings ratio. When all three indicators agree, then value estimates are likely to be reliable. When one fails to confirm the other two, look for possible distortions in the third indicator.[8]

YIELD CURVE

The study of interest rates offers a very different approach to measuring the potential for stocks over several weeks and months. In this case, you are trying to determine whether the interest rate environment is relatively favorable or hostile to the equity market, not whether the market is cheap or expensive.

A yield curve is a graphic representation of the yields of various-length Treasury securities from the three-month Treasury bill to the 30-year Treasury bond. Many analysts look at the shape of the yield curve, especially at the ratio of the yield of longer-term government bonds to the yield of shorter-term government bills or notes. On a typical graph, the three-month Treasury bill is found at the left end of the X axis, while the 30-year Treasury bond is found at the right end of that axis. Normally, the yield curve is convex in shape and rises fairly steeply from the three-month Treasury bill (in the lower left corner of a chart) to the 10-year Treasury note (in the center of that chart), and then flattens out considerably from there to the 30-year Treasury bond (on the far right of the chart).

As a rule, as the yield curve steepens (or flattens), the prospects for the stock market improve (or deteriorate). According to conventional wisdom, the critical point comes at the inflection point, i.e., the moment when the yield on the three-month Treasury bill and the yield of the 30-year Treasury bond are equal. The economy and the stock market, however, can continue to advance for several months after the yield curve inverts.[9]

Martin Zweig has developed a specific system linking stock-market performance to the shape of the yield curve. Zweig looks at the ratio of AAA corporate bonds to the Treasury-bill rate.[10] He claims that, since 1962, the annualized gain on the S&P 500 has been 5.6 percent, excluding dividends of 4 percent per year. When the ratio of the yield curve has been 1.10 or greater, the S&P has gained at a rate of 11.1 percent per year, or about double the average rate of gain. When the ratio is less than 1.10, the S&P has lost 11.2 percent per year. When the ratio is in the 1.02 to 1.10 range, however, the S&P has fallen 5.1 percent year.

When the yield curve becomes highly inverted, the impact on stock prices is even greater. When it is in the 0.88 to 1.02 range, the S&P has fallen at a 9.3 percent rate per year. When the ratio of the yield curve is below 0.88, the S&P 500 has dropped at a rate of 24.9 percent per year.

ADJUSTMENT FOR INFLATION

Although analysts usually look at nominal interest rates, there may be some danger in failing to adjust interest rates for inflation. When the yield curve inverts, high real interest rates mean that the economy will slow down relatively quickly. Low real interest rates mean that the economy will take much longer to slow down. Moreover, high real interest rates will attract money out of stocks into bonds, while low real rates of interest will attract money out of bonds into stocks. Nominal rates alone are insufficient for purposes of analysis.

For the mutual fund investor faced with a choice of stock, bond or money market funds, it might be wise to follow the lead of professional portfolio managers. Institutional investors often make asset allocation decisions based on the dividend discount model, which puts a great deal of emphasis on both interest rates and dividends. Assuming constant dividends, when real interest rates on the 30-year bond near 5 percent, many portfolio managers may want to reallocate their assets, placing more emphasis on bonds rather than stocks. Alternatively, when real interest rates on the 30-year Treasury bond reach 3 percent, professional investors may want to begin moving out of bonds into stocks. Similarly, when real interest rates on the three-month Treasury bill hit 4 percent, stocks become less attractive. When real interest rates on the three-month Treasury bill drop below 2 percent, however, stocks may become more attractive.

From October of 1990 through January of 1991, as the Federal Reserve System lowered the federal funds and discount rates, real interest rates on the three-month Treasury bill dropped into the 0 to 1 percent range. As a result, money poured into the stock market from cash-rich institutional portfolios. Belatedly, individual investors found that fixed-income investments were paying much lower rates of interest than had been the case a few years before. This led many small investors to move money from money market accounts and CDs into equity mutual funds.

GLOBAL INTEREST RATES

One factor that strongly influences foreign demand for Treasury bills, notes and bonds is competing real interest rates in various countries. Once again, analysts should adjust these rates for inflation. If real interest rates are higher in the United States than in Europe, investors will tend to sell European and buy American bonds. If real interest rates in Europe are higher than in the United States, investors will tend to sell U.S. and buy European bonds.

Analysts must also look at the trend in those real interest rates. If real interest rates in the United States are rising faster than real interest rates elsewhere (or decreasing more slowly), U.S. bonds are likely to become progressively more attractive to foreign investors. On the other hand, if real interest rates in the United States are decreasing faster than real interest rates elsewhere (or rising more slowly), then U.S. bonds are likely to become progressively less attractive to foreign investors.

EARNINGS VERSUS INTEREST RATES

Changes in real interest rates affect not only the bond market. They also have a tremendous impact on the stock market. In theory, falling interest rates lead to lower costs and improved corporate earnings. This is usually reflected in higher stock prices. Just as lower real interest rates help the stock market, rising real interest rates should hurt stock prices. The market, however, seems more responsive to declining interest rates than to rising interest rates. The reasons for this phenomenon are complex. On the one hand, Wall Street has an inherent upward bias. Stocks tend to appreciate over time. Wall Street analysts tend (correctly) to be more often bullish than bearish. Moreover, many firms can pass off rising costs to their customers and actually increase corporate earnings during periods of moderate inflation. Since gently rising interest rates have little affect on large corporations that tend to raise cash internally, a period of rising interest rates may actually benefit large companies at the expense of small companies. By contrast, declining interest rates may favor small companies whose cost of capital is substantially lower.

In the first half of 1989, for example, rising interest rates coincided with a strong bull market for the DJIA and the S&P 500. In that year, sharp increases in reported earnings offset any effect of rising interest rates for many large companies. By contrast, secondary stocks languished as their reported earnings failed to keep pace with rising interest rates. In 1991, declining interest rates coincided with a spectacular boom in secondary stocks, while large capitalization stocks lagged far behind.

These examples suggest that you need to compare the rate of change in corporate earnings to the rate of change in interest rates. A widening, positive spread between these two rates of change (either earnings are growing faster than interest rates or earnings are declining more slowly than interest rates) suggests the possibility of a market rally. A widening, negative spread between these two rates suggests the possibility of a market decline.

You also need to remember that the market responds best to its perceptions of future earnings and future interest rates and not to actual earnings and interest rates. In the summer of 1991, optimists were projecting a rally of from 3,200 to 3,500 on the DJIA, while pessimists were predicting a decline of from 2,500 to 2,700. Thus, different projections for interest rates and earnings growth resulted in wide discrepancies in stock market projections.

EQUILIBRIUM PRICE

Since projections of future interest rates and future earnings are notoriously unreliable, the average investor is better off ignoring Wall Street's wishful thinking and looking instead at current earnings and interest rates to get a rough sense of the market's potential in the immediate future.[11]

Divide corporate earnings by the current interest rate on the three-month Treasury bill. Under normal circumstances, the stock market fluctuates as much as 15 percent above or below this equilibrium value. When the market is far above the plus-15-percent level, there is excessive optimism in the market. When the market is far below the minus-15-percent level, there is excessive pessimism.

APPLYING EQUILIBRIUM THEORY: A CASE STUDY

As of 24 May 1991, the earnings on the DJIA were $151, while the three-month Treasury bill earned 5.7 percent. That gave an estimated equilibrium price of 2,649 for the DJIA versus an actual price of 2,914. Thus, the DJIA was 10 percent above its equilibrium price. If you assume that the DJIA might fluctuate between 15 percent above the equilibrium price and 15 percent below the equilibrium price, you might have expected that the DJIA could rise to 3,046 or decline to 2,252. (The maximum intraday high recorded over the following three months was 3,057.) The upper projection of 3,046 was close to a number of bullish predictions of 3,050 to 3,200 as a target price for the DJIA. The lower estimate of 2,252, however, was lower than most bearish analysts were projecting. Looking at this data in a different way, for every dollar of opportunity on 24 May 1991, there were five dollars of risk.

By the third quarter of 1991, corporate earnings on the DJIA had dropped 33 percent, while the three-month Treasury bill yielded 4.4 percent. This projected an equilibrium price of 2,289 and a maximum price of 2,632. On November 1, however, the DJIA reached an intraday peak of 3,092. This difference (i.e., 17.5 percent) could largely be explained by the fact that most analysts were expecting a 15 to 20 percent increase in corporate earnings over the next 12 months.

For a conservative, value-oriented investor, this sort of calculus suggested extreme investor optimism and a reason for caution. A rise in interest rates or a failure of the economy to respond as projected could cause a sharp decline in the DJIA. Under these circumstances, a prudent investor would begin to raise some cash, tighten stop-loss positions or hedge a portfolio through the use of futures or options.

In any case, an investor needs to use current earnings, dividends and interest rates, rather than the optimistic projections of brokerage house analysts. When P/Es, price-dividend ratios and price-to-book ratios differ substantially from historical norms, this is a reflection on the degree of investor optimism (or pessimism) about the stock market and the economy. At very high market valuations the odds favor a stock-market decline. At very low market valuations, the odds favor a rally. In between the extremes, a variety of technical indicators can help the investor decide when to buy or to sell stocks.

Endnotes

1. Robert W. Colby and Thomas A. Meyers, *The Encyclopedia of Technical Market Indicators* (Homewood, Ill., Dow Jones-Irwin, 1988), 174.
2. Colby and Meyers recommend a combination of a 7-month and a 12-month simple moving average crossover system with a dividend yield filter. When the current month-end closing price of the S&P 500 crosses above its 12-month moving average, you would go long, provided that yields were above 3.4 percent. You would close out long positions whenever the current price of the S&P 500 crosses below the 12-month moving average or yields were below 3.4 percent. When yields were below 3 percent, you would go short when the S&P 500 month-end closing price crosses below its 12-month simple moving average. You would cover short positions when the S&P 500 closes above its 12-month moving average or the yield is greater than 5.2 percent.
3. Suggested by John Bollinger on "Shop Talk," FNN, 8 September 1989.
4. Interview with Ron Insana, FNN, 20 September 1989.
5. Based on trailing book value.
6. David P. Lobell, "A Look at Book: Their Net Asset Values Say Stocks Are Too High," *Barron's,* 7 November 1988:44.
7. Some analysts claim that price-earnings ratios are affected by the underlying rate of inflation. They suggest that you should subtract the current CPI inflation rate from 20 to get the P/E multiple that can be supported at that level of inflation. This adjustment is sometimes called the "rule of 20." Thus, an inflation rate of 3 percent suggests a P/E multiple of 17 to 1, while an inflation rate of 6 percent suggests a P/E of 14 to 1. Remember, these are simply guidelines that often may be violated in practice.
8. You might apply the "rule of 20" (described in the previous note) to adjust P/Es for inflation. An interesting alternative to the traditional P/E ratio is the price to earnings before interest, taxes and depreciation (price-EBITD) ratio. This system eliminates accounting gimmickry from the equation. The price/EBITD ratio has ranged from 2.8 to 7.0 from 1959 to 1989. Unfortunately, this ratio is not readily available and requires a friendly broker working for a firm with a good research department. For details, see *Barron's,* 28 August 1989:17.
9. Ray Stone of Merrill Lynch suggests that the time between the inversion of the yield curve and a slowdown in the economy varies from 6 months to 14 months.
10. See *The Zweig Forecast,* vol. 19, no. 6 (28 April 1989): 2.

11. Ned Davis has developed a useful indicator based on the yield of the three-month T-bill and the S&P 500 stock earnings yield. Davis divides the latest 12-month earnings of the S&P 500 by its current price to get the earnings yield figure. He then compares that with the current yield on the three-month T-bill. When you have a negative spread of 0.5 percent, that's supposedly a sell signal. Over the last 23 years, Davis claims that buy signals have anticipated 14.4 percent annual increases in the S&P 500, and sell signals have anticipated 16.8 percent annual losses in that index. Fourteen of 15 trades have been profitable, and the losses on the one unprofitable trade were minor. (See *Barron's,* 27 March 1989: 26.)

5

Sentiment

Some of the most profitable market-timing systems are based on the study of investor sentiment. At first glance, sentiment seems to move the markets. Investors' selective perceptions of various political and economic factors lead to specific buying or selling decisions. In the short term, if enough investors are optimistic, they will buy stocks. This creates additional demand and forces prices up. By contrast, if enough investors are pessimistic, they will sell stocks. This creates additional supply and forces prices down. When investors become excessively bullish, that may signal an approaching market top. Alternatively, when investors become excessively bearish, that may signal an approaching market bottom. Within these extremes, however, the direction of market sentiment should be a reliable predictor of the market's overall direction.

Several different investing publics exist. We commonly think of the small, private investor and the large, institutional investor. However, there also are floor traders, specialists and members of the stock exchanges. Some of these investors are speculators, some hedgers, some **day-traders**, some short-term investors, others long-term investors. Some investors use fundamental analysis, while others use technical analysis to make their decisions. Some invest in mutual funds; others choose individual equities. Still others prefer warrants, options or futures contracts. Most investors are citizens. Some are foreigners. Each group has different perceptions of the economy and markets, different risk tolerances, different access to information and different time horizons. As a result, each behaves quite differently as a market participant.

As a rule, small investors, foreigners and large institutions have an unenviable record of buying at major tops and selling at major bottoms. Thus, they are getting out of the market at the precise time that prospects for the future are brightest and buying into the market at precisely the time when prospects for the future are the worst. When they act in concert, these wrong-way Corrigans are excellent contrary indicators.

CONTRARIAN APPROACH

In theory, when all investors agree that the market is going up, they are likely to be fully invested, waiting for someone else to push up prices. That is precisely when the market is most likely to decline as buying dwindles and a few investors begin to take profits. This sets up a wave of selling by those interested in profit taking or loss avoidance. Eventually, when all investors are convinced that the market is going down, they are likely to be fully in cash, waiting for someone else to push prices down. That is precisely when the market is likely to begin to rally as selling dwindles, a few investors close out short sales and others seek bargains. This sets up a wave of buying by those who have been on the sidelines waiting for a chance to invest.

Most analysts believe that the majority of investors, including professionals, tends to be correct when there is some difference of opinion. They tend to be wrong, however, when an overwhelming majority is convinced that the market is going up (or down).

On closer examination, sentiment appears to be a lagging indicator. Sentiment tends to improve as prices rise and tends to deteriorate as prices decline. From a purely academic point of view, sentiment indicators are the dependent variable, not the independent variable, and thus should have no direct predictive value. On the other hand, they may be treated in the same way as overbought/oversold and value indicators, i.e., as estimates of the probability that the market may change direction, rather than as causal factors. In any case, they must be used with caution in a timing system.

EXPERT OPINION

Professional investors, especially floor traders, have access to the best information on market direction. While specialists might have to make markets for customers even when they would prefer to step aside, floor traders trading for their own accounts would seem to be the most astute of all investors. Unfortunately, it is difficult to know what this group is doing on a timely basis.

Some services follow the activity of large-scale commercial traders. Supposedly, when **commercials** are buying stock and the public is selling stock, this usually marks an important market bottom. Similarly, when commercials are selling stock but the public is buying stock, this often marks an important market top. In July of 1990, the Commitment of Traders report of the Commodity Futures Trading Commission indicated that commercial traders were heavily **short** the S&P 500 and **long** the oil index—just before Iraq invaded Kuwait. The Commitment of Traders report is well worth study by technical analysts looking for a reliable, intermediate-term sentiment indicator.

Other analysts track the behavior of corporate insiders. Many analysts believe that corporate insiders possess a better grasp of how their companies are likely to do in the near future than do either investment analysts or the general public. Since 1986, however, insider buying and selling has been a less useful tool for general market timing.

In the 17 September 1990 issue of *Barron's*, Ben Turner, a senior manager with Fuji International Ltd. in London, suggested that heavy purchases of shares of stock by Employee Stock Ownership Plans (ESOPs), trusts and other corporate entities distort the data. Turner argues that if you remove these purchases, the resulting data still is quite useful.

When several different corporate insiders make a series of stock purchases in their own company over time, the chances are that stock will rally over the next several weeks and months. When several different corporate insiders are making a series of sales of stock in their own company, the chances are that this stock will decline over the next several weeks and months. When corporate insiders as a group are selling stocks, this suggests that a market top may be near. When corporate insiders as a group are buying stocks, this suggests that a market bottom may be near. Thus, the study of insider purchases and sales, which proved particularly useful throughout 1990–1991, can provide a powerful tool for general market timing. Furthermore, when the Commitment of Traders report reinforces conclusions based on insider purchases and sales data, a wise investor pays attention.

ADVISORY OPINION

The most popular of the sentiment indicators measure the opinions of professional advisers, the general public and speculators. These have been examined closely by a variety of analysts and each one has his or her own particular way of interpreting them. *Investor's Intelligence* of New Rochelle, New York, reads newsletters, calls brokers and interviews market advisers to determine how many of them are bullish, bearish or expecting a **correction**. (John Bollinger has described this as his favorite indicator.[1]) Technical analysts have devised a variety of alternate ways of using this information in their market-timing models.

One of the more reliable intermediate-term to long-term systems has been developed by William O'Neill. O'Neill regards a figure of 50 percent bearish as a highly bullish reading and 20 percent bearish as a highly bearish reading. (Alternatively, he regards 35 percent bullish as a bullish reading and 55 percent bullish as a bearish reading.) Weekly sentiment data are published in both *Barron's* and *Investor's Business Daily*. *Investor's Business Daily* also includes the high and low readings for these indicators for the past year and for the past five years, as well as the benchmarks used by most analysts to identify excessive optimism or excessive pessimism.

Investor's Intelligence data can be used in a variety of ways. John McGinley suggests that you look more closely at bullish sentiment during bull markets and bearish sentiment during bear markets.[2] Martin Zweig suggests using a 13-week moving average of bulls divided by bulls plus bears (thus ignoring those expecting a correction). John Bollinger prefers to subtract the percentage bearish from the percentage bullish and look for extremes associated with recent, intermediate-term tops and bottoms. Regardless of how you use this data, *Investor's*

Intelligence sentiment readings are an extremely valuable market-timing tool.

FUTURES TRADERS' SENTIMENT

While *Investor's Intelligence* data serves well to identify significant market moves that take three to six months to complete, other sources of data may be used to identify shorter-term fluctuations in the market lasting one to three months. One such example is futures traders' sentiment.

Futures traders are highly sophisticated professionals who employ the latest techniques in technical analysis and who have extremely short time horizons, e.g., one to two weeks.[3] The professional traders who subscribe to Future Source™[4] can follow Jake Bernstein's analysis of futures traders' sentiment on a daily basis for a wide variety of commodities. Mutual fund investors can follow the weekly data published in *Barron's* from data gathered by Earl Hadady's *Bullish Consensus*. The Hadady Corporation interviews futures traders each trading day and weights their responses according to the degree of bullishness they exhibit as well as the number of subscribers they have. This makes the *Bullish Consensus* one of the most sophisticated surveys of market sentiment available.

Earl Hadady looks at the trend of the *Bullish Consensus*. If the consensus is rising, he regards that as positive. If it is declining, he regards that as negative. (The firm uses a five-day moving average of the daily readings to smooth out minor fluctuations.) A rise in bullishness above 50 percent usually is bullish, while a decline through that level is usually bearish.

At extremes, the percentage bullish is a contrary indicator. Each market defines its own extremes. For the stock market, Hadady regards any readings above 65 percent bullish as a contrary indicator, i.e., as a time to sell stocks. Similarly, a bullish reading below 35 percent is interpreted as an indication of a major buying opportunity.[5]

Hadady claims that a failure of the *Bullish Consensus* to rise above 50 percent during a rally signals a bear market and a failure of the *Bullish Consensus* to decline below 50 percent during a decline signifies a bull market. John Murphy[6] also suggests that the 50 percent line often acts as support (during bull markets) and resistance (during bear markets). Any decisive penetration of the 50 percent line is a warning of a possible change in the fundamental direction of the market. A 5 percent reversal in the index also is a warning of a change in the market direction.

OPEN INTEREST

Technical analysts also pay great attention to volume and **open interest** on futures contracts. If the price of a contract is rising while volume and open interest are expanding, this is regarded as bullish because futures traders are establishing new long positions. If the price is rising but volume and open interest are contracting, however, this suggests that the move may be ending because futures traders are closing out previous long positions and are unwilling to establish new long positions.

Similarly, a decline in prices accompanied by expanding volume and expanding open interest is bearish because futures traders are establishing new short positions. A decline in prices accompanied by contracting volume and open interest, however, suggests that the decline may end as traders cover their shorts and are unwilling to establish new short positions.

Peter Hackstedde suggests that the real key to using the *Bullish Consensus* is to watch for extremes of sentiment accompanied by contractions in open interest on the relevant futures contract.[7]

PUT-CALL RATIO

One of the more popular indicators of short-term market sentiment is based on **options** trading and is called the put-call ratio. This indicator is particularly useful for predicting market rallies or declines over the next week or two. This ratio is computed by taking the total volume of puts and dividing by the total volume of calls.[8] There are two popular put-call ratios. One is based on puts and calls for all listed stocks on the Chicago Board Options Exchange (CBOE) and the other is based on the Options Exchange Index (OEX) of 100 stocks.

The daily put-call ratio on the CBOE usually fluctuates between 0.40 and 0.80, with an average of 50 percent. Daily spikes below 0.40 usually are associated with good, short-term selling opportunities (often within three to five trading sessions) and daily spikes above 0.80 often have been associated with good, short-term buying opportunities (again, often within three to five trading days). These parameters must be adjusted from time to time, however, to reflect changes in market behavior and investor psychology.

Note that in Figure 5.1, throughout 1988 and into early 1989, each time that the ten-day put-call ratio exceeded 70 percent, the market was at a relative low point. These would have been good buying opportunities for the average investor. Furthermore, each trough in the indicator proved to be associated with a short-term market top.

John Bollinger likes to compare the daily CBOE put volume to a ten-day moving average of itself. When the current figure is twice the moving average, you have a buy signal. Supposedly, the market is likely to rally within three to five days of such a signal. These signals are rare but are fairly reliable.

Bollinger regards the 50-day moving average as useful for capturing intermediate-term moves, i.e., more than 5 percent. (In the period 1985–1989, the market usually rallied for one to three months after the 50-day put-call ratio reached 0.70 or higher and usually sold off after the ratio reached 0.45 or lower.) Bollinger suggests using data for the past six months to a year to determine parameters for these indicators. This makes great sense.

A cautionary note comes from Alex Jacobson of the Options Institute. Jacobson suggests that two-thirds of all options' volume comes from arbitrage-related programs.[9] Thus, he regards most put-call ratios as unreliable—except at extremes. Jacobson claims that Shearson Lehman Brothers, Inc., and Merrill Lynch and Co. use a very accurate call-put ratio based on public buying of options. He claims that these ratios provide very good statistics. Unfortunately, they are not readily available to the general public.

FIGURE 5.1   Ten-Day Put-Call Ratio, February 1988 to April 1989

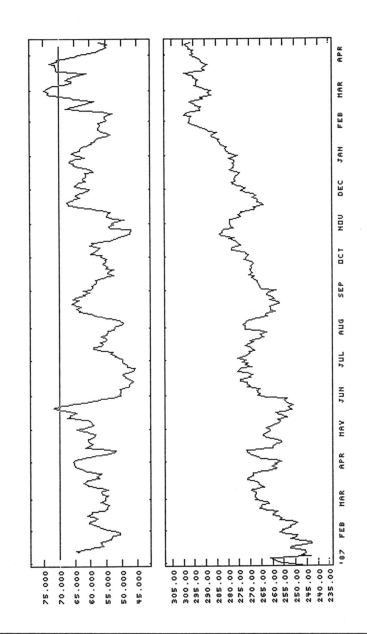

MOVING AVERAGES OF CALL-PUT RATIO

Most people find it easier to interpret a call-put ratio than the usual put-call ratio. When the call-put ratio is large, it reflects optimism. When it is small, it reflects pessimism. A double-crossover system using a 5-week and a 13-week moving average of the data provides a very useful intermediate-term market-timing indicator. When the 5-week **simple moving average** (SMA) crosses above the 13-week SMA, you have a buy signal. When the 5-week SMA crosses below the 13-week SMA, you have a sell signal.

PUT-CALL PREMIUM RATIO

George Moldenhauer of the *Long and Short Report* claims that when **premiums** on put options are extremely high relative to the premiums on call options, professional investors are selling the options while the public is buying put options.[10] This suggests to Moldenhauer that the likely course of the market is upward, not downward.

The put-call premium ratio is more useful as an intermediate-term timing tool and the ten-day put-call ratio is more useful as a short-term timing tool. The ten-day put-call ratio is a useful complement to the put-call premium ratio, however, and tends to confirm its signals at major tops and bottoms.

ANSBACHER INDEX

The problem with sentiment indicators based on put and call options is that there are too many possibilities, not too few. One very useful, straightforward approach that simplifies the problem for the average investor is the Ansbacher index. Max Ansbacher looks at the call-put premium ratio based on out-of-the-money calls and puts. He uses the premium on index options that are approximately 15 points out of the money. For example, if the S&P 100 currently is at 400, Ansbacher would look at the price of the 415 call versus the 385 put. Supposedly, a neutral reading is reflected in a ratio of 0.80 to 1.20.

Readings that are much higher than 1.20 suggest that the market is willing to pay an excess premium for call options and, therefore, is excessively bullish. Readings much below 0.80 suggest that the market is willing to pay an excess premium for puts and, therefore, is excessively bearish.[11] Fortunately for the average investor, the ratio is easy to calculate and CNBC/FNN follows the index on a regular basis.

ODD-LOT SHORT SALES

Several sentiment indicators supposedly examine the behavior of small investors. **Retail customers,** as a group, have the least training and the worst access to information of all market players. As a result, they tend to react slowly to new trends and they have been used as contrary indicators by the experts. The popularity of mutual funds may distort somewhat the usefulness of traditional sentiment indicators based on odd-lot statistics.

Some critics argue that most odd-lot short sellers today are professional traders and that the amateurs are trading OEX puts and calls. On the other hand, some evidence still suggests that odd-lot short sellers have a particularly poor record of picking market tops and bottoms. Thus, when the number of odd-lot short sales increases substantially as a proportion of all odd-lot sales, e.g., above 4 percent, this has been regarded as a mistake on the part of uninformed small-scale speculators and is regarded, contrarily, as a buy signal. When odd-lot short sales as a percentage of all odd-lot sales decline to below 0.5 percent, this usually is regarded as marking an important market top and should be taken as a warning of a possible decline.

Some very serious problems, however, have been associated with the standard treatment of odd-lot sales. According to Laszlo Birinyi, odd-lot sales have exceeded odd-lot purchases for all but one day during the 1982–1988 bull market.[12] On the surface, that seems incredible, perhaps impossible. Instead of questioning whether the data measures what analysts think it measures, most analysts conclude that odd-lot players have been consistently wrong. Logic suggests, however, that these statistics must be misleading. Small investors cannot consistently sell stocks without buying them in sufficient quantity to balance their sales. Odd-lot statistics are distorted by round-lot purchasers who often sell smaller quantities of shares in odd lots. Thus, any indicators based on odd-lot statistics should be used with extreme caution. Nevertheless, odd-lot short-sales statistics are a particularly useful indicator of market rallies and, to a much lesser extent, of market declines. Other indicators, however, particularly the mutual fund redemption-sales ratio and the American Association of Individual Investors (AAII) survey of small investors, seem to be far more useful for measuring the relative bullishness or bearishness of small investors.

MUTUAL FUND REDEMPTIONS AND SALES

One of the best indicators of small investor sentiment is found in mutual fund data. Small investors who lack the expertise to pick stocks, whose resources are inadequate to purchase a broadly diversified portfolio of individual stocks or who fear manipulation by unscrupulous brokers tend to purchase various mutual funds for their investments. The most aggressive of these investors might short Fidelity's mutual funds or switch their investments back and forth from equity to money market funds. The more conservative of these investors might just buy (or sell) mutual funds as they perceive great opportunity (or risk) in the stock market. An increase in mutual fund purchases by investors is a sign of optimism. An increase in sales of mutual funds by investors is a sign of pessimism. The ratio of mutual fund purchases to mutual fund sales appears to be a lagging indicator with some potential to be used as a contrary indicator when that ratio is at extremes.

Clearly, the surge in sales of mutual funds in 1987 was a sign of public speculation in stocks often associated with market peaks. Few technical analysts, however, paid much attention to this data. Instead, they clung to well-established measures of speculation by the public, including odd-lot data. In 1988, sales of mutual funds by investors, called redemptions, remained at about the same level as in 1987. Purchases of mutual funds by investors (called sales in the Investment Company Institute's statistics published weekly in *Barron's*), however, lagged far behind 1987. This indicates a buyers' strike. After a good first quarter in 1988, the ratio of purchases to sales in the second quarter of 1988 increased—suggesting that small investors had become more optimistic.

INSTITUTIONAL CASH

Stock-market analysts pay close attention to the amount of cash in institutional hands. Institutions dominate the market. Lack of money to invest is negative for the market, while abundant cash is positive. Financial reporters talk frequently about the markets being awash with cash when brokerages, pension plans, mutual funds and other institutions have large amounts of money at their disposal. Many analysts follow the statistics on mutual fund cash published by the Investment Company Institute Research Department. Published in *Barron's*, these monthly statistics are labeled Liquidity Asset Ratio (Equity). Excess cash held by mutual funds is a useful indicator of potential demand in the marketplace. Unlike money supply data that has a much greater lead time, mutual fund cash data is likely to be tied much more closely to significant trends in the market. It also is a contrary indicator because a high level of mutual fund cash indicates bearishness among fund managers and a low level of cash indicates bullishness among fund managers.

Unfortunately, the interpretation of this data is subject to wide disagreement. Some experts will claim that there is a lot of cash in institutional hands at the same time that other experts claim that cash levels are relatively low. How can we resolve this dispute?

EXCESS MUTUAL FUND CASH INDICATOR

Norman Fosback has developed a sophisticated mutual fund cash indicator that is an improvement on raw percentages. As interest rates rise, mutual fund managers are ever more hesitant to invest in stocks and are more likely to purchase commercial paper with excess cash. Thus, purchase of commercial paper represents a relatively riskfree source of income and competes with common stocks for the fund's assets. Fosback takes the figure published by the Investment Company Institute Research Department and subtracts a constant of 3.2 percent, i.e., the minimum cash he claims is needed for operating capital. He also adjusts the data for the current commercial paper rate. Fosback uses a factor of 0.7 to multiply the commercial paper rate to further reduce his estimate of excess cash. The remainder is the excess cash held by mutual funds and is a good measure of their buying power. According to Fosback, while excess cash above 2 percent is bullish, 2.5 percent is extremely bullish. (The mutual fund cash position also may serve as a good substitute for an estimation of excess institutional cash.)

Unfortunately, mutual fund cash data is released three weeks late and Fosback's constant of 0.7 may need occasional revision. You might find it easier to follow the INDATA reports of mutual fund cash and to compare current levels of cash to levels at previous market highs and lows. If current levels of institutional cash are at or near the levels seen at previous intermediate-term market bottoms, the market outlook is relatively favorable. If cash levels are similar to those at recent intermediate-term market tops, the market outlook is relatively unfavorable.

CASH-REDEMPTION RATIO

Martin Pring uses the ratio of total mutual fund cash to a three-month total of redemptions to signal whether the mutual funds are experiencing cash shortages because of redemptions. The theory is that high ratios, i.e., 18 to 1 or greater, suggest that sufficient excess cash exists to fuel a major rally, while ratios below 8 to 1 suggest that mutual funds are strapped for cash and may not have much buying potential.

AMERICAN ASSOCIATION OF INDIVIDUAL INVESTORS (AAII) SURVEY

Mutual fund cash data is a monthly statistic released after several weeks' delay. A more timely measure of small investor sentiment is a weekly survey conducted by the American Association of Individual Investors (AAII). Each week, the AAII polls its members and classifies them as bullish, bearish or expecting a correction. You might recalculate the bullish figure as a percent of those who are either bullish or bearish, i.e., those who have a definite opinion. For short-term trading purposes, i.e., for one to three months, a reading of 60 percent or above on this revised index often has been a sign of a significant, short-term market top and a reading of 40 percent or below often has been a sign of a significant, short-term market bottom. If you calculate a ten-week simple moving average of the revised index, you can create a very useful oscillator as the difference between the weekly reading and the ten-week moving average.

DISAGGREGATE APPROACH TO MARKET SENTIMENT

Investors must pay close attention to the time horizon of various sentiment indicators. Major market moves often occur when long-term sentiment is extremely optimistic or pessimistic, rather than when short-term or intermediate-term sentiment is at an extreme. Changes in market prices of 30+ percent are more likely to occur when price-dividend ratios or price-earnings ratios are at an extreme. Approximately 10 to 20 % changes are likely to occur when the 50-day Open Arms index (discussed in Chapter 8) or advisory sentiment indicators are at an extreme. Smaller moves of 5 to 10 percent are likely when short-term indicators such as the ten-day Open Arms index or futures traders' sentiment are at an extreme.

FALSE CONTRARIANS

Because the herd often is wrong at extremes, many analysts like to call themselves contrarians. By this, they mean that they do the opposite of what the crowd is recommending. There is a problem with such claims, however. Some people say they are contrarians when they really are afraid to admit that they agree with the majority. Fear of being identified with the crowd introduces an element of noise into sentiment indicators. Robert Nurock suggests that a distinction should be made between active and passive sentiment, between what people say and what they do. Data from such surveys as the AAII, *Investor's*

Intelligence or the *Bullish Consensus* tell you what people are saying. Indicators such as the put-call ratio, the put-call premium ratio, the mutual fund sales-redemption ratio and the odd-lot short-sales ratio tell us what traders and investors actually are doing.

Endnotes

1. Response to a question by Liebe Geft on "Shop Talk," FNN, 28 September 1989.
2. Interview with John Bollinger, FNN, 6 December 1988.
3. This impression is corroborated by an interview on FNN with Craig Corcoran of the *Futures Hotline* by Gary Salem, 8 December 1988. Corcoran indicated that his service limits its predictions to the next one to two weeks.
4. Future Source™ is a service of Oster Communications in Cedar Falls, Iowa.
5. "Shop Talk," FNN, 22 June 1989.
6. John Murphy is the chief technical analyst for CNBC/FNN as well as the author of a superb book, *Technical Analysis of the Futures Markets* (New York: Prentice-Hall, 1986).
7. "Market Wrap," interview with Bill Griffeth, FNN, 20 February 1990.
8. "The Options Report," interview with Bill Griffeth, FNN, 29 November 1988.
9. "The Options Report," Interview with Bill Griffeth, FNN, 21 November 1989.
10. Interview with Richard Saxton, FNN, 22 November 1989.
11. Interview with Jennifer Bauman, FNN, 7 February 1991.
12. "Wall Street Week," 2 September 1988.

6

Charts and Moving Averages

Technical analysts pay great attention to price charts to gain insight into the character of the stock market. Chart analysis also is used for individual stocks, bonds, currencies, precious metals, commodities, mutual funds and market indexes. Critics of technical analysis scoff at chartists and love to point out how analysts can be tricked into thinking that an electrocardiogram actually is a stock chart with a remarkable cyclical component. Despite the criticism and ridicule, however, chart analysis is the stock-in-trade of the technical analyst.

Three basic types of charts exist: bar charts, point-and-figure charts and candlestick charts. Bar charts usually have a price scale on the Y axis and a time scale on the X axis. Each day's high, low, opening and closing price is included for that day.[1] While all three types of charts have their advocates, bar charts are the easiest for most investors to interpret and use.

BAR CHARTS

Bar charts consist of a vertical line that represents the difference between the highest and the lowest prices recorded for that stock or index for a specific day, week or month. Usually, a small horizontal line to the left of the vertical line represents the day's opening price. A small horizontal line to the right of the vertical line represents the day's closing price. Technicians are interested in the relationship between all four characteristics of the day's price movement: open, close, high and low. They also are interested in the relationship between several days' patterns, as well as between price action and total volume. Bar charts also lend themselves to the use of moving averages and oscillators in trading systems. Many chartists, as they are called, base their decisions to buy or sell exclusively on the basis of these charts. It takes a long time to be able to make much sense out of charts. This skill is essential, however, if you want to be successful as a market timer or short-term trader.

POINT-AND-FIGURE CHARTS

Point-and-figure charts also have a price scale on the Y axis, but there is no time scale. Instead, the X axis represents changes in market direction. Each time the market is rising, a series of ascending Xs are put into vertical boxes. When the market reverses direction and starts to sell off, the chartist moves one column to the right and enters a series of descending Os in vertical boxes just to the right of the column of Xs.[2]

Point-and-figure charts are regarded as especially useful as a means of identifying entry and exit points, stop losses and the size of a move likely to occur. These charts can be used in exactly the same way as bar charts. They can be constructed using hourly, daily or weekly data. They make extensive use of support and resistance lines, as well as various formations such as triangles, the double top or bottom, the triple top or bottom and the head-and-shoulders top or bottom. (In the case of point-and-figure charts, however, support and resistance lines always are drawn at 45-degree angles.) Congestion areas are horizontal areas where prices have moved back and forth several times. Supposedly, the width of the congestion area on a point-and-figure chart provides a rough estimate of the probable move up or down once a breakout has occurred (see Figure 6.1).

Chart formations trace the history of recent investor optimism (or pessimism), as well as the relative balance of buyers and sellers at specific price levels. Whether they have predictive value remains problematic. Technicians are quick to point out the need for confirmation of chart signals from a variety of indicators.

While bar charts are easier for most people to interpret, point-and-figure charts have the advantage of very specific rules for making

FIGURE 6.1   Point-and-Figure Chart, June–November 1990

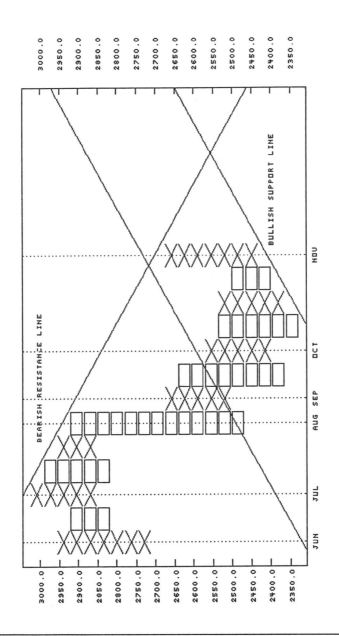

trades. The choice between these two systems is more a matter of how well you can understand and interpret either type.

SPECIAL CHART FORMATIONS

Technical analysts pay special attention to triangles that take several weeks to form. Ascending triangles are characterized by rising bottoms and flat tops. These supposedly are bullish formations. Descending triangles have flat bottoms and declining tops. Supposedly, these are bearish formations. Symmetrical triangles have declining tops and rising bottoms. With triangles, a breakout is expected about two-thirds of the way to the apex. The amount of the move expected from this formation is determined by the width of the base, i.e., the distance between the start of the lines of support and resistance that form the horizontal lines of the triangle. Add (or subtract) the base from the breakout point to identify a price target. With triangles, volume should contract as you move toward the apex and then expand on the breakout.

Expanding triangles are rare and usually are associated with tops in the market. They have increasing volume over time and it is hard to choose points to establish long or short positions. Rectangles are similar formations with flat tops and bottoms. Usually, volume is fairly steady. This formation also is called a trading range. Picking points for new long or short positions is relatively easy.

Small flags and pennants usually are formed within a few days to a week or so and often are continuation patterns. Normally, the flag or pennant slopes in a direction contrary to the major trend. When the flag or pennant slopes in the direction of the major trend, this suggests a reversal formation. Normally, the distance between the previous breakout and the pennant or flag is the size of the move expected after the pennant or flag is completed.

JAPANESE CANDLESTICK CHARTS

The Japanese have developed a method of charting stocks and commodities that is based on the relationship between high, low, opening and closing prices. In this system, the area between the opening and closing price is filled in to create what the chartists call a main body.

Above this main body, a thin line extends to the daily high, and below this main body, a thin line extends to the daily low. These are called shadow lines. When the opening price is lower than the closing price, i.e., an up day, the main body is colored with red ink. (If you use computer software to generate these charts, the main body is white, not red, as in Figure 6.2.) When the opening price is higher than the closing price, i.e., a down day, the main body is colored with black ink.

The Japanese look at days in which the opening price is the low for the day and the closing price is the high for the day as very strong days. (Alternatively, the Japanese look at days in which the open is the high and the close is the low for the day as very weak days.)

If a long, main body has a single shadow line, this is considered a fairly strong up day (red or white body) or down day (black body). If a short, main body has two, short, equal shadow lines, this is considered a possible turning point. If the opening price is the same as the closing price and there are two, long, equal shadow lines, this is considered an even more likely sign of a turning point.

If there is a short, main body with a long, lower shadow, then the market is considered very strong (if this occurs near significant support) or very weak (if this occurs near significant resistance).

Fortunately for those familiar with American bar graphs, the Japanese candlestick method is similar to its American counterpart. In both cases, technicians look for M tops and W bottoms, head-and-shoulders formations, price gaps, island reversals, inside days, outside days, etc. Both look for confirmation of chart patterns from volume. But there are some significant differences in the ways in which the Japanese approach their candlestick charts that provide additional insight into the market.

Clearly, the focus on the main body places attention on the relationship between the opening and closing price that is not so systematically explored in American bar-charting methods. Also, this method is particularly useful in identifying reversal days, whereas traditional Western methods of analysis are more useful for trend identification.

For the purposes of pattern recognition, the Japanese candlestick-charting method is the most precise method we have, other than the

FIGURE 6.2   Candlestick Chart, January 1991

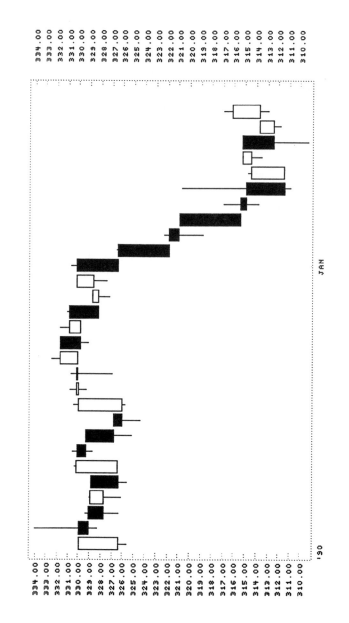

Elliott Wave system. Developed by R. N. Elliott, the Elliott Wave system attempts to identify repetitive patterns in stock-market prices.[3] This system is extremely popular with many analysts. Unfortunately, the four best-known or the current practitioners (A. J. Frost, Robert Prechter, Glenn Neeley and Mike Drakulich) do not always agree on their "wave count," i.e., which part of which wave has just occurred. If the experts are confused, so too is the ordinary investor. By contrast, Japanese candlestick charts are more susceptible to systematic testing by large computers.

TEN-DAY CLOSE-OPEN (C-O) LINE

If you find candlestick charts confusing, you can construct a ten-day simple moving average of closing prices minus opening prices. This is a linear approximation of the information contained in the main body. Compare that close-open (C-O) line to the price chart, looking especially for divergences. In June of 1990, the C-O line declined for almost a month, while closing prices on the DJIA rose steadily. This warned of the possibility of a sell-off ahead. Then, in July, the market entered a cyclical bear market that took the popular averages down by more than 20 percent. In February of 1991, the same divergence was noted as the DJIA corrected sideways for three weeks. The C-O line provides additional information not contained in either bar charts or point-and-figure charts. Thus, it is a useful addition to the basic internal strength indicators used by analysts.

An analyst might find it very useful to combine Japanese candlestick charts with conventional Western trend-following techniques such as moving averages, support and resistance levels, trend lines, etc. Contrarians and those using oscillator-based overbought/oversold systems also could use candlestick charts profitably.

SUPPORT AND RESISTANCE LEVELS

During a period of general advance, the stock market may stall for a few days or weeks. The failure to break above a specific level is said to create a resistance level. (The failure to break below a specific price is said to generate a support level for a given stock or index.) The more the market (or stock) tests that resistance level, the more significant the eventual breakthrough is regarded.

During a period of general decline, the market may stall for a few days or weeks. The point at which a market decline is halted is correctly called resistance by analysts. This use of language, however, often confuses average investors. Thus, in this book, we will refer to resistance as downward pressure preventing further rallies and support as upward pressure preventing further decline.

For many years, 1,000 on the Dow was an important psychological resistance level. Later, 2,000 was seen as important. In 1990, 3,000 was a key level. If resistance levels are penetrated on a sudden surge of volume, technicians regard the new move as confirmed. (Some analysts suggest that a doubling of volume as compared to the recent five-week average daily volume is an important and useful rule of thumb.) If volume declines, however, then the penetration is regarded as unlikely to prove significant. Similarly, during a period of general decline, when the market stalls for several days or more at a particular price level, this is regarded as support for the market. The longer the market refuses to penetrate that level, the more significance is attributed to that support level. After the penetration of that support level, the old support level is regarded as potential resistance to any renewed rally. Similarly, an old resistance level, once penetrated, is regarded as potential support during any renewed decline. This seems to be one of the more useful forms of chart analysis.

CORRECTIONS

Market analysts love to talk about corrections. Corrections are simply interruptions in the major trend in the market. They can take one of two major forms: corrections in time or corrections in price. If the stock market is rising strongly and then spends a few days or weeks going nowhere, this is a correction in time. If prices fall, however, this is a correction in price. If the market has been declining steadily, then a sideways movement for several days or weeks is a correction in time, while a rise in prices is a correction in price.

Many analysts consider 33 percent, 50 percent or even 66 percent retracements of previous rallies or declines as normal. A 33 percent correction suggests that the previous trend is likely to resume with force, while a 66 percent correction suggests that the current trend is weakening and may be on the verge of reversal. Other analysts use Fibonacci numbers as targets for corrections. (Fibonacci was a 13th-century Italian mathematician who identified a series of numbers where the next number is the sum of the two previous numbers, e.g., 1, 2, 3, 5, 8, 13, 21, 34, 55, 89, 144, etc. These numbers also have an additional characteristic. Starting with the sixth number, you can create a ratio of $N/(N+1)$ that approximates 0.618.) Analysts who use Fibonacci numbers look for retracements of 38.2 and 61.8 percent of the previous move. To date, little systematic research supports stock-market applications of Fibonacci numbers. Selective perception on the part of traders may be responsible for the excessive confidence placed in those numbers.

Despite this criticism, at times, the Fibonacci numbers seem to work. For example, Figure 6.3 contains a combination of two indicators, an Andrews pitchfork and Fibonacci arcs. The Andrews pitchfork was drawn using three consecutive extreme points (low-high-low). The highest point and the lowest point are connected by an invisible line that is then bisected by the third point. Two other lines are then drawn parallel to this middle line with their origins at the other two points. The upper line represents upside resistance, the lower line represents downside support. The middle line provides resistance to any rally. Fibonacci arcs are drawn using the distance between the most recent high (or low) and a subsequent low (or high). Curved lines are then drawn at a distance that represents 38 percent, 50 percent and 62 percent retracements of the previous move. Note also that one Fibonacci arc intersects with the Andrews pitchfork at the extreme right of the chart—suggesting that a breakout above the 2,680 to 2,700 range would be very bullish for the market. This indicates the possibility of a rise back to the 3,000 level. Such a breakout did occur in late January of 1991 and was followed by a rally back to 3,000 in March.

FIGURE 6.3   Andrews Pitchfork and Fibonacci Arcs, June–
December 1990

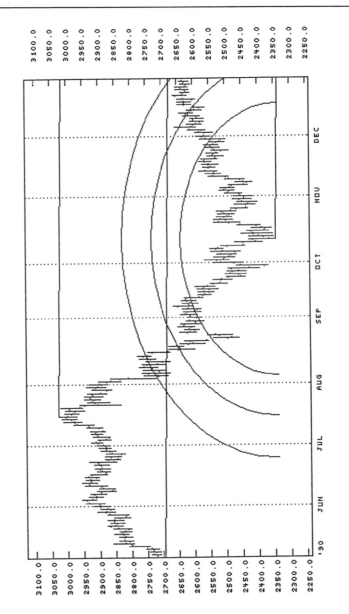

RANGE EXPANSION

John Bollinger suggests that you pay particular attention to what happens as the market violates previous support or resistance levels. He looks particularly at whether the range of daily prices (high minus low) expands during the move. If so, he regards this as a sign that the move is likely to continue. This concept is a useful addition to traditional chart analysis based on support and resistance levels.

SPEEDLINES

Speedlines are support (or resistance) lines drawn from the starting point of a move through its highest (lowest) point. Then you divide the total point move into thirds and construct lines that trisect that move. During a bull-market correction, you would expect the market to decline to the first speedline. Any penetration of this speedline means that the second speedline becomes the target. Penetration of the second speedline means that the entire move is likely to be retraced. This approach is particularly useful in strongly trending markets where conventional chart analysis fails to identify important levels of support and resistance.

During market declines, any rally is likely to hit the first speedline. Any penetration of the first speedline identifies the target as the second speedline. Any penetration of the second speedline suggests that the entire decline may be retraced. This system supplements support and resistance levels identified by chart analysis and facilitates the identification of target prices for both rallies and declines.

TREND CHANNELS

Trend channels are formed by parallel lines of support and resistance. During bull markets, the support line usually serves to identify the lower level likely to be reached during short-term corrections. The resistance line usually serves to identify the upper level likely to be reached during short-term market rallies. If a rally breaks through a resistance line of an up-channel, that suggests that an even more bullish phase of the market rally is beginning. If, by contrast, the market breaks through the support level of an up-channel, an early warning of a possible change in market direction is given.

Similarly, during bear markets, you would expect rallies to reach the upper (i.e., resistance) level of a down-channel and sell-offs to reach the lower (i.e., support) level of the down-channel. If a rally breaks through the upper level (the resistance level), this provides an early warning that the decline soon may be over. A breakdown through the lower level (i.e., the support level of the down-channel), however, is a sign of even more bearish conditions ahead.

A more subtle warning is given when the market refuses to reach a resistance level (the upper line) during a rally. This suggests that the rally may be losing strength. During a decline, failure to reach a support level (the lower line) indicates that the sell-off may be losing strength. In Figure 6.4, the fact that the rally in August of 1987 to all-time highs failed to reach the upper trendline was a preliminary warning of possible trouble. The violation of the lower trendline in early October of 1987 signaled the start of a precipitous decline. Thus, careful study of trend channels is a very useful form of chart analysis and can be used to anticipate trend reversals long before they occur.

MOVING AVERAGES

Many primitive trading systems are based on various-length, simple moving averages of closing prices. Among the most widely followed are the 20-day, 50-day and 200-day moving averages (see Figure 6.5). Most of these use daily closing prices on a major index (or individual stock). Moving averages also are used for advance minus decline, up volume minus down volume and new highs minus new lows data.

A commonly used technical trading system for long-term investors is based on the 200-day moving average. You buy stocks or mutual funds whenever that 200-day average is penetrated to the upside by the current closing price of the stock, mutual fund or index. You sell stocks or mutual funds whenever the 200-day moving average is penetrated to the downside by the current closing price of the stock,

FIGURE 6.4   Up-Trending Channel, January–November 1987

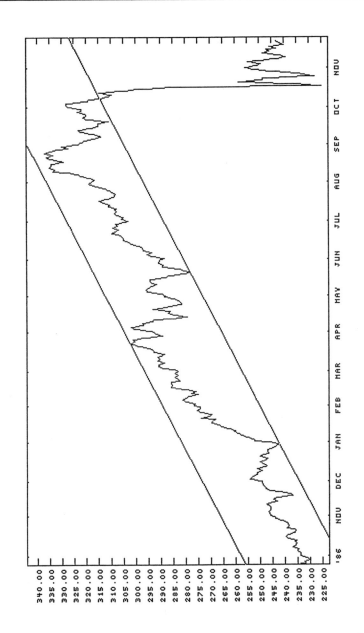

mutual fund or index. A critic of moving averages, Michael Hayes, claims that:

> A number of empirical tests of the moving-average trading strategy have been conducted using both individual stocks and market indexes. Although some of the studies have found evidence of systematic behavior in prices, and, therefore, lend support to the price-trend assumption, the invariable conclusion is that the moving-average trading strategy produces investment results that are *worse* than random timing.[4]

Some traders use filters and trading rules to try to avoid being whipsawed in fluctuating markets. Thus, they might require a 3 percent penetration of the moving average and/or two days of closing prices above (or below) the moving average before they regard that penetration as generating a valid signal. Those interested in the intermediate trend often use 50-day exponentially weighted moving averages, while short-term traders use 19-day to 21-day simple moving averages of price indexes.

Mutual fund investors might find all these options a bit bewildering. What, then, can we conclude? At best, all moving-average systems tend to bring you into the market after a rally has started and get you out after the peak has been passed. Moving-average systems, however, do seem to have some ability to capture part of the move in strongly trending markets. When used appropriately, moving averages are one of the most useful powerful tools for the study of price, volume, breadth, leadership and sentiment in the market.

DOUBLE-CROSSOVER METHOD

One favorite method of using moving averages is to buy stocks whenever the current price closes above a specific moving average and to sell stocks short whenever the current price closes below the same moving average. This is sometimes called a double-crossover system. It often is used with 20-day, 50-day and 200-day moving averages. Naturally, all moving-average systems work best in trending markets and work worst in trendless markets. (In trendless markets, oscillators

FIGURE 6.5   20-Day, 50-Day and 200-Day Moving Averages, June–
December 1990

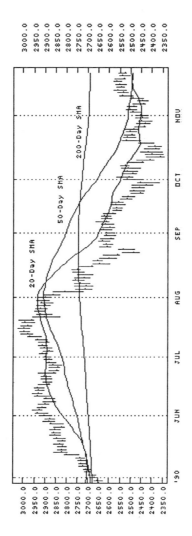

seem to work best.) For example, in Figure 6.6, a 65-day SMA of daily closing prices of the Nikkei 225 would have provided an excellent example of a double-crossover trading system.

FORTY-FIVE-WEEK MOVING-AVERAGE/ TREASURY-BILL SYSTEM

John Bollinger has developed a timing model that seems to improve substantially over the standard moving-average system. His model consists of a 45-week moving average of the S&P 500 and a four-week moving average of the three-month Treasury-bill rate. By adding an interest-rate indicator to a moving-average system, many of the whipsaws in other moving-average systems are eliminated.

The system works as follows: When you are out of the market, buy when the Dow closes above the 45-week moving average *and* the three-month Treasury-bill rate has declined over the past four weeks. When you are in the market, sell whenever the Dow closes below the 45-week moving average *and* the three-month Treasury-bill rate has increased over the past four weeks. Under all other conditions, hold your current position unless the moving average is violated by 3 percent or more.

Bollinger also says that a breakdown below the lower 3 percent band or a breakout above the upper 3 percent band gives a continuation signal, i.e., that the first signal is renewed and that the current move is expected to continue further (see Figure 6.7). Bollinger claims that this model would have returned 14 percent per year over the past 20 years.

EXPONENTIAL MOVING AVERAGES

Another method of calculating moving averages involves exponential transformation.[5] Exponential moving averages seem more responsive to current data than arithmetic moving averages. The use of exponential forms of the average or ratio also will cut down on the number of whipsaws. A simple method to approximate an exponential moving average is to transform raw data by using a smoothing constant equal to two, divided by the number of days plus one. For ten days,

FIGURE 6.6   Nikkei 225 with a 65-Day Moving Average, February–
October 1990

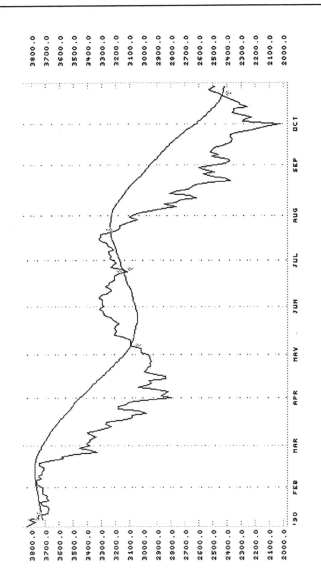

FIGURE 6.7 Forty-Five-Week Moving Average of the DJIA Plus
3 Percent Trading Bands, March 1990 to March 1991

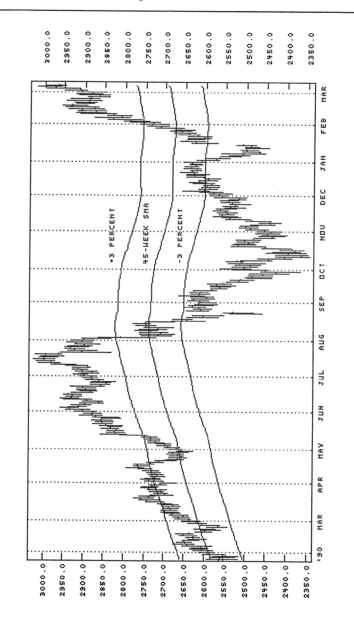

the constant is 0.18. For 50 days, the constant is 0.04. Multiply the newest data by the constant and add the old data multiplied by one minus the constant. (In the case of the ten-day averages, the constants would be 0.18 for the new data and 0.82 for the old data.) Exponential moving averages are particularly useful with advance minus decline, up volume minus down volume and new highs minus new lows data where day-to-day changes can cause sharp jumps in moving averages that may be misleading.

Endnotes

1. Steve Nison of Merrill Lynch Capital Markets has published a superb book entitled *Japanese Candlestick Charting Techniques: A Contemporary Guide to the Ancient Investment Techniques of the Far East* (New York: New York Institute of Finance, 1991).
2. The best book on this system is Michael Burke's *The Three-Point Reversal Method of Point and Figure Chart Construction and Formations* (New Rochelle, N.Y.: Chartcraft, 1990).
3. The most readable book on the Elliott Wave system is by A. J. Frost and Robert Prechter, *Elliott Wave Principle: Key to Stock Market Profits* (Gainesville, Ga.: New Classics Library, 1990).
4. Michael Hayes, *The Dow Jones-Irwin Guide to Stock Market Cycles* (Homewood, Ill.: Dow Jones-Irwin, 1977), p. 89. *See also* Paul H. Cootner, "Stock Prices: Random vs. Systematic Changes," in *Frontiers of Investment Analysis*, pp. 489–510, as cited in Hayes.
5. These have the additional advantage of transforming curvilinear data into linear data for the purposes of analysis with multiple regression programs.

7

Price Indicators: The Bête Noire of the Efficient Market Hypothesis

Technical analysts have developed a great number of technical indicators based on hourly, daily, weekly or even monthly price data. These include such things as moving averages, trendlines, chart patterns and momentum indicators. Analysts claim that using these indicators can lead to very profitable trading. On the surface, however, profitability tests do not seem to justify the enthusiasm of the experts.

Appendix I contains a series of standard profitability tests on six popular indicators: the directional oscillator, 20-unit simple moving average, moving average convergence-divergence, stochastics, 12-day price momentum indicator and the parabolic stop-and-reverse system. (This last indicator was developed by Welles Wilder. It is used primarily by futures and commodities traders who want to be constantly invested in the markets on either the long or short side and who have a relatively short time horizon for their individual trades.) Profitability tests were generated using MetaStock Professional 2.0™[1] for the DJIA from 17 March 1989 to 8 March 1991. Only one out of six of these systems turned a profit (5.2 percent), while the DJIA rose 9.9 percent. The rest lost varying amounts of money. How do we reconcile the enthusiasm of the experts for these indicators versus the dismal record of performance charts in this two-year test?

At one level, there is a tremendous difference between trading on the basis of indicator signals alone and trading based on a combination of an indicator and a stop-loss system. As Bruce Babcock points out in his book, the *Dow Jones-Irwin Guide to Trading Systems*, traders can make a very healthy profit even if their signals are right only 40 to 50 percent of the time, provided that they cut their losses short and let their profits ride. Most simple profitability tests do not include the stop-loss systems used by traders.[2]

At another level, the performance of technical indicators improves markedly if you disaggregate your data. Some indicators work best in trending markets, while others work best in oscillating markets. Used at the right time, even a simple moving average such as the 65-day SMA used in conjunction with the Nikkei 225 in 1990 (as in Figure 6.6) could be extremely profitable. Used at the wrong time, e.g., the DJIA in 1988, such a system would have been a disaster! How do you know when to use either one? Professional traders can tell after a quick glance at a price chart whether a trend-following or an oscillating system would be more appropriate. For the average investor who lacks that experience, something more mechanical is needed. One very useful approach was developed by J. Welles Wilder, Jr., and is called the directional movement system.

WELLES WILDER'S ADXR

The ADXR is part of Wilder's directional movement system. This system is used to select specific stocks or commodities to trade and it also provides explicit buy and sell signals. The calculations of these indicators are beyond the scope of this book but are contained in Section IV of Wilder's book, *New Concepts in Technical Trading Systems*. These calculations also are available through a variety of technical analysis programs that are available commercially.

Wilder defines directional movement as "the largest part of today's range that is outside yesterday's range."[3] Wilder's Directional Indicator (DI) is the ratio between the positive (or negative) directional movement from day one to day two, divided by the true range over that period. The true range is defined as the largest of three measurements: today's high minus today's low; today's high minus yesterday's close; or today's low minus yesterday's close.[4]

Wilder's Plus Directional Indicator (+DI) is the sum of positive directional movement over a specific number of days (usually 14) divided by the true range for that period. His Minus Directional Indicator (-DI) is the sum of the negative directional movement over that period, divided by the true range. Wilder states that "true directional movement is the difference between $+DI_{14}$ and $-DI_{14}$."[5]

The Directional Movement Index (DX) is the difference between $+DI_{14}$ and $-DI_{14}$ divided by the sum of the two. The Average Directional Movement Index (ADX) is the smoothed 14-day moving average of the DX. Today's DX is added to the DX for 14 days ago and divided by two. To compute the ADXR, you smooth the ADX over 14 days.

When the ADXR is above 25, the market has a strong trend. In this case, trend-following indicators should provide good market-timing signals. When the ADXR is below 20, the market has a weak trend. In this case, oscillators should provide good market-timing signals. Two things should be remembered about the ADXR. First, when it is between 20 and 25, it does not provide clear signals. Second, you need at least 56 days of data before the $ADXR_{14}$ becomes reliable.

BOLLINGER BANDS

Perhaps John Bollinger's greatest contribution to technical analysis to date has been his system of volatility bands based on a 20-day simple moving average. He calculates both the moving average and the standard deviation for the first 20 days. He then plots the moving average for day 20 along with parallel bands at a distance of two standard deviations. Each day, he continues plotting the moving average and the standard deviation bands, dropping day 1 and adding day 21. (Day 2 becomes day 1 and day 21 becomes day 20, etc.)

When the market closes above its 20-day simple moving average, this is bullish. When it closes below its 20-day simple moving average, this is bearish (see Figure 7.1). When the market reaches the plus-two standard deviation band, the market is overbought. When the market reaches the minus-two standard deviation band, it is oversold. Often, the market can remain overbought or oversold for considerable periods of time. If the market continues to travel along the upper band, it is extremely bullish. If it continues to travel along the lower band, it is extremely bearish. When the market closes outside the second standard deviation band, this is a continuation signal. When the market touches an outer band and then recedes toward the moving average on the next

FIGURE 7.1   Bollinger Bands with a 20-Day SMA, November 1990
to January 1991

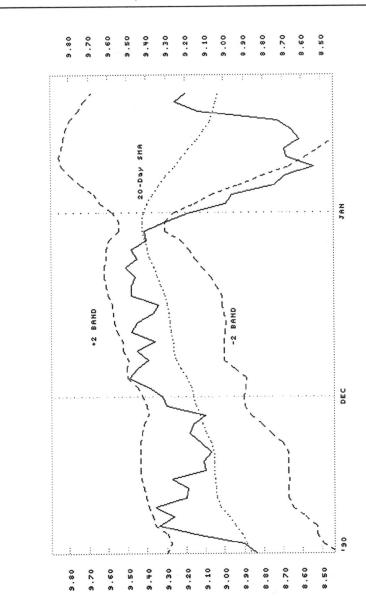

trading day, however, this warns the investor of a possible reversal ahead.

Bollinger bands work extremely well with a variety of stocks, bonds, mutual funds, indexes, etc. For the short-term trader, Bollinger bands based on a 20-day moving average and used in conjunction with George Lane's stochastics (to be described later in this chapter) work extremely well. For the intermediate-term trader, Bollinger bands based on a 65-day moving average along with Welles Wilder's Relative Strength Index (RSI) (also to be described later in this chapter) work well. For the long-term trader, a 195-day moving average along with Bollinger bands seems quite useful. In this case, however, you should use RSI based on weekly rather than daily data.

Bollinger's system also provides an empirical set of targets based on market volatility. In general, a market is expected to oscillate between the plus-two and minus-two standard deviation bands around its moving average. Depending on the length of the moving average, e.g., 20, 65 or 195 days, Bollinger bands provide short-term, intermediate-term or long-term price objectives, respectively. It is important to remember, however, that several days or weeks of sideways action can reduce the amount of price decline (or rise) necessary to meet the targets established by the volatility bands.

MOVING AVERAGE
CONVERGENCE-DIVERGENCE (MACD) SYSTEM

Among the newer tools of technical analysis is the moving average convergence-divergence system or MACD. Developed by Gerald Appel, a highly successful intermediate-term market timer,[6] MACD is based on exponential moving averages. MACD provides an indication of the market trend, early warnings of a possible change in direction and explicit buy and sell signals.

As explained by Alexander Elder,[7] you create a 12-period exponential moving average or EMA (smoothing constant = 0.15) and a 26-period exponential moving average (smoothing constant = 0.075). Subtract the 26-period average from the 12-period average and plot the difference. Then, calculate a nine-period exponential moving average (smoothing constant = 0.2) of the new data and plot it as well.

When the faster moving line crosses through the slower moving line (the nine-period EMA), you get buy and sell signals. You get a simple buy signal when the faster line crosses above the nine-period EMA, and you get a simple sell signal when the faster line crosses below the nine-period EMA (see Figure 7.2). Elder also suggests using histograms of the same data. He says:

> MACD lines indicate the direction in which the crowd is running. The MACD histogram tracks the enthusiasm of the crowd. It measures the difference between shorter and longer moving averages and extends when the crowd is more enthusiastic. When the MACD histogram shrinks and flattens out, you know the crowd is running out of steam; it is time to begin looking for a reversal of the trend.[8]

You also can look for divergences between the MACD histogram and the price index. For example, if the MACD histogram makes a series of lower highs while the Dow makes a series of higher highs, this is a negative divergence suggesting a sell-off in the near future. Similarly, if the MACD histogram makes a series of higher bottoms while the Dow makes a series of lower bottoms, then you might expect a rally in the next few days.[9]

Technicians are enthusiastic about MACD because it can be used several ways. You can look for divergences between MACD and closing prices. You can use MACD as a momentum indicator. You can identify lines of support or resistance. Buy signals can be generated when MACD penetrates above a downwardly sloping resistance line, the difference crosses above a nine-day EMA of itself and/or both lines cross the zero line to the upside. Sell signals can be generated when MACD penetrates below an upwardly sloping support line, the difference crosses below a nine-day EMA of itself and/or both lines cross the zero line to the downside.

This system is multifaceted. You can combine it with an overbought/oversold indicator to cope with extremes within trending markets. In any case, MACD suffers from the common problem of all trend-following systems in that it does not do so well in trendless markets.

FIGURE 7.2   Nova Fund and MACD, November 1990 to March 1991

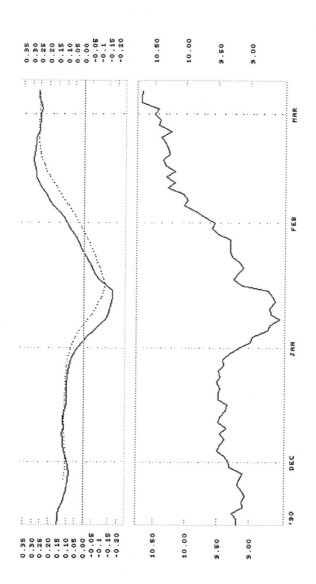

PRICE MOMENTUM INDICATORS

Many technicians believe that changes in momentum precede changes in market direction. This would seem to be a truism. Momentum seems to fall off before a top is reached and before a bottom is reached. Some markets, however, may experience upside blowoffs or V-shaped bottoms and suddenly trend very strongly in the opposite direction without any warning from momentum indicators. Nevertheless, loss of momentum usually is an early warning signal of a possible change in the market direction.

To create a simple momentum indicator, divide today's closing price by the closing price x number of days ago, e.g., ten days. A ten-day price momentum ratio often warns of possible market tops at readings of 1.05 or higher and warns of possible market bottoms with readings of 0.95 or lower (see Figure 7.3). Martin Pring uses longer-term price momentum indicators such as 13, 26 and 52 weeks to reveal changes in the primary trend. He uses the slope of these lines to confirm the current trend and the inflection point to confirm a turning point.[10]

Price momentum indicators help the investor to identify the extent to which a given market has run out of gas or is picking up momentum. Momentum indicators are particularly useful in trading-range or oscillating markets but are less useful in trending markets. In oscillating markets, they often warn of an imminent correction in price. In trending markets, they often warn of a correction in time.

WELLES WILDER'S RELATIVE STRENGTH INDEX

My favorite momentum indicator is the Relative Strength Index (RSI). Developed by Welles Wilder, RSI has proven popular with analysts studying stocks, mutual funds, market indexes and commodities. Although Wilder used the past 14 days of price data to calculate this **overbought/oversold** indicator, others have used his system on 5-day, 9-day, 14-day, 21-day and 28-day intervals.

The average of points gained during up days is divided by the (absolute value of the) average of points lost during down days over the past 14 trading days (the average of days up divided by the average of days down). That ratio then is inserted into the standard oscillator

FIGURE 7.3   OTC Indexed Fund and Ten-Day Price Momentum
Indicator, October 1990 to March 1991

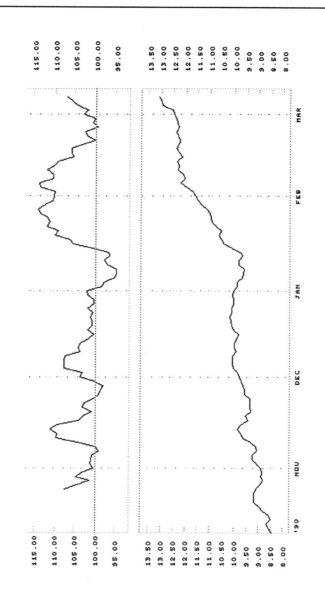

formula: $100 - (100 \div (1 + F))$, where F = the formula in question. During a major up trend, when the ratio reaches 80, the market is reaching overbought territory, and when it reaches 40, it is reaching oversold territory. During a sideways market, when the ratio reaches 70, the market is reaching overbought territory, and when it reaches 30, it is reaching oversold territory. During a major down trend, when the ratio reaches 60, the market is reaching overbought territory, and when it reaches 20, it is reaching oversold territory.

When the oscillator first reaches overbought (or oversold) territory, this is simply a warning to start looking for a selling (or a buying) opportunity. Markets can stay overbought (or oversold) for prolonged periods of time. Look for divergences between the broader market average (or stock or mutual fund) and its RSI. The December 1989 to January 1990 period and July 1990 offer excellent examples of bearish divergences in Figure 7.4. Likewise, the August–October 1990 period offers an excellent example of a bullish divergence.

If the RSI is in overbought territory and the stock or index breaks out to a new high but the RSI does not, this is a bearish divergence. Thus, if the Dow is making a series of higher highs but the RSI is making a series of lower highs, then the technician anticipates a trend reversal in the Dow. The actual sell signal, however, is generated when the RSI rises above the appropriate criterion level and then drops back through that line to the downside (80 percent in up trends, 70 percent in sideways markets and 60 percent in down trends). Similarly, if the RSI is in overbought territory and the stock or index drops to a new low but the RSI does not, this is a bullish divergence. After the market gets oversold and there is a bullish divergence between the RSI and the price index, the actual buy signal is generated when the RSI drops below the appropriate criterion level and then rises back through it to the upside (40 percent in up trends, 30 percent in sideways markets and 20 percent in down trends). It appears that the RSI is similar to simplified price momentum indicators but provides a much more sophisticated set of trading signals.

FIGURE 7.4 Minnesota Mining and Manufacturing with a 14-Period
Relative Strength Index, April 1989 to October 1990

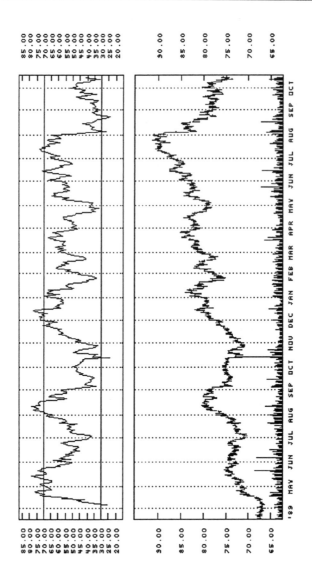

RELATIVE STRENGTH

The concept of relative strength is quite different from that of Wilder's RSI. Relative strength refers to the performance of a specific stock, group or index relative to some reference group (see Figure 7.5). For example, *Investor's Business Daily* publishes a relative strength rating in percentiles for each stock listed on the major exchanges. Various stock pickers, including Dan Sullivan of the *Chartist* and David Ryan of *Investor's Business Daily,* use relative strength as a very important criterion for selecting stocks for investment. Similarly, *Growth Fund Guide* uses relative strength for its selection of mutual funds. Sullivan selects stocks whose relative strength is at or above the 90th percentile level for his newsletter. In addition, Sullivan prefers stocks costing more than $30 and avoids low-priced stocks that, he says, have a poorer success rate than more expensive stocks. He claims that with these two screens, he has achieved a 75 percent success rate with his picks. As a rule, during bull markets, small investors should trade stocks, mutual funds and indexes with high relative strength, e.g., that are above the 80th percentile.

STOCHASTICS

Stochastics are momentum oscillators designed to measure the relationship between daily closing prices and the range of daily prices. Stochastics assume that prices tend to close nearer to the top of their trading range in rising markets and closer to the bottom of their trading range in declining markets. Usually, signals from stochastics occur earlier and more frequently than signals from the RSI.

Compute a basic oscillator called the %K, which subtracts the minimum price over the past five days from today's closing price. Divide that remainder by the range over the past five days. Next, compute the %K-Slow, which is a three-day moving average of the %K. Finally, compute the %D-Slow, which is another three-day moving average, based on the %K-Slow. Graph the %K-Slow and the %D-Slow and trade as the faster %K-Slow crosses the %D-Slow line.

Interpreting stochastics is fairly simple. When the slower of the two lines, the %D-Slow, crosses into an extreme zone (e.g., above 75

FIGURE 7.5 Relative Strength (Boeing versus DJIA), May 1989 to May 1990

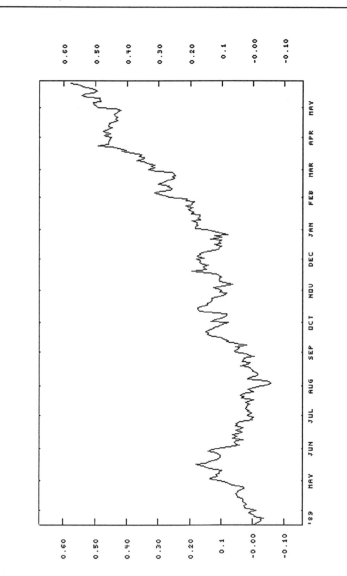

to 85 percent or below 15 to 25 percent), a preliminary warning is given. Then, when the faster %K-Slow line crosses the slower-moving %D-Slow line, the actual signal is triggered. Perry Kaufman suggests that these two lines function in a way similar to two moving averages.[11] This system works best in trendless markets with high volatility.

In Figure 7.6, a five-day stochastic gave a buy signal in the NYSE Financial Index in mid-January of 1991 and a much less profitable sell signal in mid-February of that year. The long period in which the stochastic traded above the 80 percent level suggests that the Financial Index was in a strong bullish trend.

Although stochastics can be created rather easily for a single stock, there are some problems when you try to use stochastics, Larry Williams's %R[12] or Marc Chaikin's volume accumulator (discussed in Chapter 8) with stock index data. The published highs and lows in the financial press are theoretical highs and lows for the day. The high prices reached during the day for all stocks in the index are calculated to give a theoretical high. The low prices for each stock are used to calculate a theoretical low for the index. Yet, at no time that day did the index trade at either the theoretical high or the theoretical low. John Bollinger regards these theoretical numbers as almost worthless and suggests that, instead, you use the print highs and lows.[13]

When stochastics and the RSI conflict, Bollinger suggests that stochastics should be regarded as the shorter-term indicator.[14] For example, if stochastics are suggesting a possible rally yet the RSI is suggesting a possible sell-off, you might look for a short-term bounce followed by a more significant decline in the market.

George Moldenhauer suggests that the most useful aspect of stochastics is how long the market stays in an overbought or oversold condition.[15] If the market tends to stay overbought for a fairly substantial period but stays oversold only for a brief period, this is bullish for the market. By contrast, if the market stays oversold for considerable periods of time but remains bullish only for brief periods, this is bearish for the market.

The *Encyclopedia of Technical Market Indicators* regards stochastics as unreliable. The profitability test included in Appendix I would seem to bear out that conclusion. When markets are in a trading range, however, stochastics are very useful. During strongly trending phases of the market, stochastics can generate a number of poor signals. This

FIGURE 7.6   NYSE Financial Index and Slow Stochastics, January–
March 1991

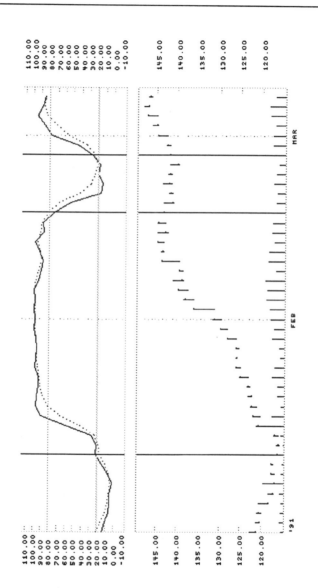

is a classic example of the importance of using the right tool at the right time.

INVESTOR'S INTELLIGENCE
MOMENTUM INDICATORS

Another very popular indicator is based on the percentage of stocks above their 10-week and 30-week moving averages. *Investor's Intelligence* calculates these two momentum indicators each week. These indicators emphasize the relative performance of individual stocks versus their own recent price history. Reported weekly by Michael Burke in *Investor's Intelligence*, a reading of 70 percent of all stocks above their 10-week (or 30-week) moving average is a preliminary warning of an overbought market. When that figure then drops below 70 percent, a sell signal is generated. Burke claims that such a decline suggests a possible decline of approximately 5 percent in the market. Similarly, when fewer than 30 percent of all stocks are above their 10-week (or 30-week) moving average, this is a preliminary oversold signal. When that figure rises above 30 percent, a buy signal is generated. During strong rallies, corrections are likely to end when the 10-week moving average hits the 50 percent level. Presumably, during strong declines, rallies are likely to end at the 50 percent level. This indicator has a particularly good track record.

Dan Sullivan claims that the percentage of stocks above their 30-week moving averages is an extremely useful indicator of major bear markets.[16] Sullivan says that when the percentage of stocks above their 30-week moving average rises from below 60 percent to above 80 percent and then declines below 60 percent, this indicator has predicted a bear market in 10 out of 11 cases.

DOW JONES MOMENTUM INDICATOR

A similar indicator has been developed by Jim Gaspar of Merrill Lynch in Los Angeles based on the 30 stocks in the DJIA.[17] When all 30 stocks are above their individual 39-week (alternatively, their 200-day) moving averages, this is a major sell signal. Conversely, this is a major buy signal. Gaspar claims that this system has caught all the important market tops and bottoms for as long as he has been keeping the data.

CYCLE THEORIES

Although there are a great number of analysts who study stock-market **cycles**, most academicians regard cycle theory with great skepticism. On the other hand, among the ranks of economists are a number of cycle theorists, including such noted scholars as W.W. Rostow and W. Arthur Lewis.[18]

Both Rostow and Lewis argue for the existence of a 3-year (Kitchin), a 9-year (Juglar), a 20-year (Kuznets) and a 50-year cycle (Kondratiev). Rostow has identified various-length business cycles, including such things as a short-term inventory cycle and a very long-term residential construction cycle.[19] He explains that "irregularities in the pattern of growth derives from lags and from distortions in the process of investment away from its optimum sectoral paths."[20]

He says further that

these distortions arise from three factors: Investment decisions tend to be determined by current indicators of profitability rather than by rational long-range assessments; these indicators tend to make many investors act in the same direction without taking into account the total volume of investment in particular sectors that is being introduced by current profit expectations; and, beyond these technical characteristics of the investment process, there is, psychologically, a follow-the-leader tendency, as waves of optimism and pessimism about the profits to be earned in particular sectors sweep the capital market and industries where profits are (or are not) being plowed back in the expansion of plant.[21]

He concludes:

In theory, during a business expansion, the interaction of the multiplier and the accelerator proceeds in a cumulative, self-reinforcing process until full employment of labor or some other physical bottleneck is reached. This sets a ceiling on the level of output. The accelerator, which gears investment to the rate of increase in output, then turns investment downward. Through the multiplier, investment and output fall. Through the accelerator, investment declines further. . . . A theoretical floor is reached when gross fixed investment falls to zero. Investment and income cease to decline. The excess capital stock has been worked off. The continued rise in population and continued flow of technological possibilities with the passage of time now make investment and the expansion of capital stock profitable again; investment expands; and the interaction of the multiplier and the accelerator yields a new cumulative cyclical expansion.[22]

As various sectors of the economy overshoot (or undershoot) their optimum levels of capitalization, these sectors enter cycles of varying length, depending on the rate of capital accumulation in that sector. The longer it takes to create excess investment, the longer the cycle and, presumably, the longer the time it takes to purge a sector of its excesses.

Rostow's analysis thus provides a theoretical basis for cycle theory. The cycles perceived by technical analysts are, perhaps, the result of the interaction of multiple investment cycles of varying length, some of which cancel each other out and others of which reinforce one another. Such common concepts as a **nesting of cycles** suggest a series of cycles that come together without interference by a larger, more powerful cycle. **Cycle inversion**, however, suggests that these smaller cycles are overwhelmed by the coincidence with an opposite phase of a much more powerful cycle. **Cycle extension** suggests that a series of smaller cycles has coincided with a more powerful cycle perhaps not analyzed by the technician.

Cycle analysis is a very difficult and often subjective art that is beyond the capabilities of the average investor. The great danger in cycle analysis is that, as with the Elliott Wave theory, analysts are hard-pressed to specify why specific cycles are supposed to persist in the future.

SIMPLIFIED APPROACH TO CYCLE ANALYSIS

Craig Corcoran of the Davis-Zweig Futures Hotline has described a simple method of making annual forecasts based on a composite cycle built from three different cycles.[23] Corcoran uses the ten-year, or decennial, cycle, the four-year presidential-election cycle and the one-year seasonal cycle for his annual predictions. Once you have identified the probable trends for the year, try to identify the most recent lows of the 13-week cycle and project these dates out for the new year. Split these periods in two for an approximate date for the 6.5-week cycle.

Sophisticated, computer-based financial analysis programs, such as MetaStock Professional 2.5™, often contain time-series analysis.[24] With MetaStock 2.5, you get fast Fourier transform. Using Fourier transform, you should be able to identify the three strongest cycles in a data series. This should allow you to be much more precise in your short-term market analysis. In time, you may begin to see patterns that are, hopefully, actually there. Just be careful.

SEASONAL CYCLES IN INDIVIDUAL STOCKS

Little doubt, there are cycles within the price-chart patterns of many individual stocks. Most of these are related to fluctuations in the seasonal demand for those products and to the release of quarterly earnings reports.

For example, Coca-Cola stocks seem to peak in the late summer and trough in the early winter. McDonald's and other fast-food chains seem to have two peaks per year, i.e., in summer and around the Christmas holidays. Kodak stock seems to peak in the summer. In each of these cases, you could make a strong case for seasonal demand for that product influencing cycles in the prices of those stocks.

Endnotes

1. MetaStock™ is a product of Equis International in Salt Lake City, Utah.

2. Victor Sperandeo's book, *Trader Vic—Methods of a Wall Street Master* (New York: Wiley & Sons, n.d.), is a particularly good example of how successful traders operate.

3. J. Welles Wilder, Jr., *New Concepts in Technical Trading Systems* (Greensboro, N.C.: Trend Research, 1978), p. 36.

4. Ibid.

5. Ibid., p. 39.

6. Mark Hulbert identified Appel's *Systems and Forecasts* as the top market-timing newsletter for the past four years in *Forbes* (12 November 1990): 362.

7. Alexander Elder, "How to use MACD to catch price trends early," *Futures* (September 1986): 68–70. *See also* "Using MACD and MACD-histograms," *Futures* (May 1990): 36.

8. Ibid., p. 70.

9. Dr. Alexander Elder, interview with Bill Griffeth, FNN, 6 February 1989.

10. Martin J. Pring, *Technical Analysis Explained*, 2nd ed. (New York: McGraw-Hill, 1985), pp. 107–8.

11. Perry Kaufman, ed., *Technical Analysis in Commodities* (New York: Wiley & Sons, 1980), p. 100.

12. This system compares the daily close to the range of prices over a fixed number of days. This scale is inverted, however, with an overbought reading above 20, while an oversold reading is below 80. As a result of this inversion, the %R is harder for most people to use than stochastics and gives almost identical signals.

13. Comment made in response to a viewer question on "Shop Talk," FNN, 22 September 1989.

14. "Shop Talk," FNN, 22 June 1989.

15. Interview with Richard Saxton, FNN, 20 September 1989.

16. "*Investor's Daily* Business Show," interview with William O'Neill, FNN, 21 August 1989.

17. As discussed in *John Bollinger's Capital Growth Letter*, 18 February 1991.

18. W. Arthur Lewis, *Growth and Fluctuations, 1870–1913* (Boston: Allen & Unwin, 1978).

19. W. W. Rostow, *The World Economy: History and Prospect* (Austin: University of Texas Press, 1978). Reprinted by permission of the author and the University of Texas Press.

20. Ibid., p. 307.

21. Ibid., pp. 307–8.

22. Ibid., p. 308.

23. Interview with Gary Salem, FNN, 29 December 1988.

24. This version of the program requires a hard disk.

8

Seeking a Second Opinion: Internal-Strength Indicators

While a few technical analysts would trade stocks based only on the behavior of price indicators, most prefer to look at market breadth, leadership and volume for confirmation of buy and sell signals. These are the so-called internal-strength indicators.

ADVANCES AND DECLINES

Perhaps the most popular of the internal-strength indicators are those based on market breadth. One analyst, Mark Forney, depends entirely on advance-decline data for his market-timing model. Typically, analysts look at the total number of shares advancing on the NYSE and compare that number to the total number of stocks declining on that exchange each day. Some analysts prefer to look at both numbers in terms of all the shares traded that day, i.e., advances, declines and unchanged.

CUMULATIVE ADVANCE-DECLINE (A-D) LINE

One simple example is the cumulative advance-decline (A-D) line, which is created by taking the number of shares advancing each day, subtracting the number of shares declining and adding that total to the previous day's total. This cumulative A-D line then is compared to the behavior of stock-market prices to seek confirmation of the current price move. When price movement is confirmed by the cumulative A-D line, technicians are convinced that the current move will continue. When price movement is not confirmed by the cumulative A-D line, analysts become concerned that the current trend in prices may reverse.

While many analysts believe that the cumulative advance minus decline line has good forecasting potential, there is a downward bias in that line. The prices of advancing stocks seem to rise more, on an average, than prices of declining stocks fall. Thus, caution must be exercised when using this indicator.

In 1987, the A-D line failed to confirm new highs in the Dow after March of that year. On the other hand, a similar bearish divergence in May and June of 1990 properly warned of an impending decline. As indicated in the data for December 1990 in Figure 8.1, even a brief divergence between the cumulative A-D line and the price series often can warn of an impending short-term change in the market direction.

When combined with the testimony of traditional value indicators, the cumulative A-D line provided ample and early warning of a possible market top. A long divergence between the cumulative advance minus decline line and the Dow in 1988, however, proved misleading as prices rallied strongly throughout the first three quarters of 1989. In general, the testimony of the A-D line should not be ignored unless you have overwhelming evidence to the contrary.

In your analysis, be careful not to confuse the A/D line with the A-D line. The difference is that with the A/D line, you divide advancing stocks by declining stocks, whereas with the A-D line, you subtract declining stocks from advancing stocks. The first creates a ratio, while the second creates a difference. The interpretation of ratios creates special problems in conjunction with the Arms index, which is discussed later in this chapter.

TEN-DAY MOVING AVERAGE

In addition to the cumulative A-D line, a ten-day cumulative advance minus decline line is very useful for short-term market analysis. Some analysts have suggested that the ten-day line tends to reverse itself at +/- 2,500. This provides an additional over-bought/oversold indicator.

FIGURE 8.1 Advance Minus Decline Line Confirmation, August 1990 to March 1991

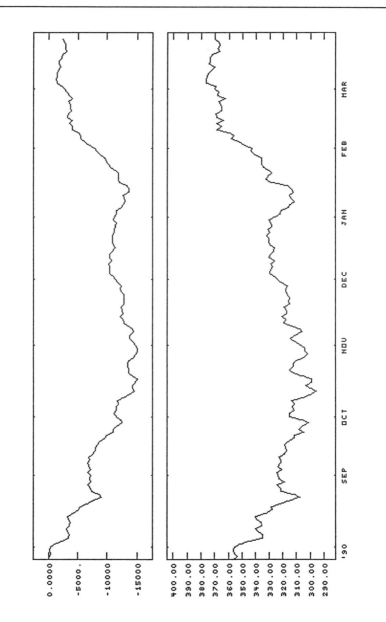

John McGinley has studied various forms of the advance minus decline line and claims that the most reliable method is to take advances divided by advances plus declines over a ten-day period.[1] McGinley claims that this indicator provides good insight into market behavior over the next five trading days. Thus, when the indicator is positive, the market outlook is positive, and when the indicator is negative, the market outlook for the next week is negative. McGinley asserts that this indicator has statistically significant results.

PLURALITY INDEX

Another popular variant of the advance minus decline line is the Plurality index described by Michael Hayes in the *Dow Jones-Irwin Guide to Stock Market Cycles*. Hayes uses the absolute value of the difference between advancing issues and declining issues on a daily basis and then divides that number by the total number of issues traded that day. He then creates a ten-week moving average of the data to generate buy signals. The index normally varies from 20 to 30 percent. Low readings are usually characteristic of broad, spreading tops, whereas high readings often indicate selling climaxes. Readings of 40 to 50 percent are associated with major cycle bottoms, according to Hayes. This was true in 1962, 1966, 1970 and 1974. Unfortunately, the index gave two false signals in 1973.

McCLELLAN OSCILLATOR

Among the more sophisticated measures of an overbought or oversold market, Sherman McClellan's oscillator is widely used by market technicians. Steven Todd of the *Todd Market Timer* regards the McClellan oscillator as his favorite market-timing tool.[2] You calculate 5 and 10 percent exponential moving averages of the daily difference between advances and declines. Then you subtract the 5 percent average from the 10 percent average and plot the difference. When that difference reaches +100, the market is overbought on the short term; when that difference reaches -100, the market is oversold. Although this is not a true oscillator, because readings can exceed +/- 100, it usually takes on the appearance of an oscillator. Normally, you expect the market to rebound from extreme overbought or oversold readings within three days to three weeks. There are other ways to use this indicator, however. For example, Bollinger prefers to use divergences between price action and the McClellan oscillator to generate buy and sell signals.

Kennedy Gammage suggests that small changes, i.e., those from zero to four points from one day to the next, suggest the possibility of a significant move.[3] This is especially true when the McClellan oscillator hovers between plus five and minus five. Under these circumstances, there is an 82 percent chance of a significant move and a 71 percent chance that this move will be in the direction of the oscillator's movement.[4] Gammage also says, however, that several of these small moves in a row cancel each other out.[5] Thus, for example, from 13 July to 16 July 1989, the McClellan moved from +38 to +41 to +38 to +38, yet Gammage said this meant nothing.

On other occasions, Gammage has suggested that readings between +30 and -30 are in the neutral range, while readings above or below that zone are overbought or oversold, respectively. Readings above +70 and below -70 are significantly overbought or oversold and readings above +100 or below -100 are regarded as extremely overbought and oversold, respectively.

Gammage further suggests that major buy signals are identified by the McClellan oscillator by the formation of a complex bottom that has oversold readings approaching the -70 to -100 range, followed by a penetration of at least 15 points above the zero line and then a decline to negative readings. This decline should constitute a higher low on the chart than the initial move to the -100 territory. He calls this a buy-spike. The McClellan oscillator then should cross the zero line to give a major buy signal.[6]

Gammage insists that buy-spikes have occurred at nearly every major bottom and at about 95 percent of important intermediate-term market bottoms since 1962.[7] These buy-spikes usually are followed by a six-week to eight-week rally. Gammage also plots fan lines on the 10 percent exponential moving average to generate buy and sell signals.[8] Typically, the violation of the third fan line signifies a change in direction of the market. The McClellan oscillator is an improvement over the simple ten-day advance minus decline line and provides a much more explicit set of rules to determine how much the market may be overbought or oversold.

SUMMATION INDEX

The Summation index is simply a running total of daily readings of the McClellan oscillator. If the slope of the Summation index is positive, the market outlook is bullish. If the slope is negative, the outlook is bearish. Changes in the shape of the Summation index often give timely warnings of significant changes in the market direction.

Peaks and troughs in the Summation index seem to be coincident with peaks and troughs in the broader market averages. The fact that the broader market often declines before the blue chip averages, however, gives the Summation index some forecasting value for those invested in funds indexed to the S&P 500, the DJIA or the OEX. Gammage suggests that intermediate-term traders and those trading mutual funds use the Summation index rather than the McClellan oscillator for their trades.[9] As the Summation index turns upward, go long. As it turns downward, sell stocks.

Gammage says that in a bear market, the Summation index often declines to -1,500 or lower. Then, a rally in that index to 2,000 or higher indicates the start of a new bull market. He also has said that when the Summation index reaches over +/− 2,000, the market is likely to reverse direction. Gammage suggests that when the Summation index drops below zero, the market is falling apart.[10] Thus, the zero line represents an important threshold in his analysis.

NEW HIGHS AND LOWS

Martin Pring, Stan Weinstein, Joe Granville and Justin Mamis have emphasized the usefulness of looking at new highs and new lows to identify market tops and bottoms. Mamis has called the new highs minus new lows line the "single best indicator for years—for decades."[11] When the market hits a new high, many stocks should be reaching new highs and few hitting new lows. Conversely, when the market hits a new low, many stocks should be hitting new lows and few hitting new highs. Deviations from this pattern are signs of transitions in the major trend. When used in conjunction with the cumulative advance minus decline line, this indicator suggests the extent to which a move in the Dow is shared by the broader averages.

Joe Granville considers the number of stocks making new 52-week highs a very important indicator of major stock-market tops and the number of stocks making new 52-week lows a major indication of major stock-market bottoms.[12] Granville claims that major tops occurred in 1978 and 1987 when the number of new highs dropped by more than 80 percent from their peak. He claims that the market never has failed to correct substantially each time the number of new highs has dropped by at least 80 percent. Conversely, Granville claims that he felt sure that the crash of 19 October 1987 was a major buying opportunity because the number of new lows hit that day was at an all-time high.

An alternative approach to identify a major market top is Norman Fosback's High-Low Logic index. Fosback takes the smaller of the weekly number of new highs and new lows and then divides this number by the total number of issues traded. When this ratio exceeds 7 percent, a sell signal is generated. While Fosback uses a five-week moving average, Gerald Appel recommends using the weekly data. In either case, major market tops supposedly are characterized by a large number of both new highs and new lows that occur at the same time.

One way to identify market bottoms has been suggested by Bernadette Murphy who looks at the number of new lows as a percentage of all issues traded.[13] When that percentage is equal to or greater than 15 percent, you have an intermediate market bottom. When that percentage is equal to or greater than 30 percent, you have a major market bottom.

For the average investor, an easy way to interpret new highs minus new lows data is to construct a simple moving average of the data and use that high-low line to look for confirmation or nonconfirmation of the price trend. The ten-day new highs minus new lows line tends to lag the market. Thus, the five-day SMA is preferable.

VOLUME

Tom Aspray has suggested that

Volume . . . is an essential tool in analyzing chart formations. In an up trend, volume should increase on up days and decrease on down days. In a decline, volume should be heavier on down days and should be lighter on up days. If volume acts in contrary fashion, the current trend should be viewed with suspicion.[14]

Despite claims to the contrary, volume would seem to be a classic example of a coincident indicator. Research suggests that volume tends to expand on rallies and to contract on declines. Most technicians, e.g., Stan Weinstein, William O'Neill, John Bollinger, et al., compare price behavior to volume trends to determine whether the current market move is likely to continue or whether it is likely to exhaust itself soon. They pay attention to what happens to volume as stocks reach new highs or new lows. On breakouts above resistance levels, if volume increases dramatically for a few days, this supposedly is a sign that the trend may continue. If volume remains constant or drops off, the new move is likely to prove short-lived. On breakdowns below support levels, increased volume is less necessary to confirm the move. A sudden acceleration in volume, however, may suggest a selling climax.

It is a mistake to discount low volume during a market sell-off. Low volume is strongly correlated with market sell-offs, just as high volume is strongly correlated with market advances. Low volume may be best thought of as a buyers' strike in which prices decline as sellers have difficulty soliciting attractive bids. On the other hand, declining volume during a sell-off is a sign of a dwindling supply of sellers and this is constructive for the market.

Great enthusiasm for a stock can lead a series of would-be buyers to bid up the price of that stock as a series of investors, who have made a profit, sell out at successively higher prices. When prices are falling, however, a rush to sell the stock reflects a profound pessimism among the holders of the stock, which is likely to infect potential purchasers and keep them out of the market. Thus, except for short sellers, a selling frenzy eventually has to run out of fuel, whereas a buying frenzy can feed on itself for a much longer period of time.

TOTAL VOLUME

A simple yet effective way to study volume is to construct a simple moving average of daily total volume for a specific number of days and then compare that total volume line to prices. Among the most popular are moving averages of 10, 20 and 50 days. A ten-day moving average of cumulative volume is particularly useful for short-term market timing. Thus, if prices are climbing but the ten-day SMA of total volume refuses to confirm that rally, that is a negative sign.[15] This is a fairly useful indicator, but Joe Granville's on-balance volume indicator is a substantial improvement over total volume.

ON-BALANCE VOLUME

Among the technicians who believe that volume is a leading indicator of price movement, Fosback and Granville insist that changes in volume are followed by changes in price. Widely followed by many analysts, the on-balance volume (OBV) indicator is calculated using the total volume for each trading day. When prices are up for the day, Granville adds the total volume to the previous total. When prices are down for that day, Granville subtracts the total volume for that day.

Volume accumulators belong in the trend-following category along with the cumulative advance minus decline line and the long-term moving average systems. You analyze volume accumulators and cumulative advance minus decline lines using basic chart analysis, looking for divergences between prices and the accumulator—or for signs of reversal, bottoming or topping action.

Regression analysis suggests that changes in the on-balance volume indicator (based on the NYSE) is strongly correlated with changes in the Dow, just as one would expect it to be. The question is whether the indicator can be used to predict future trends in the Dow. Critics point out that this indicator is most useful when it diverges from the current trend of the market.

VOLUME ACCUMULATOR

Marc Chaikin has developed a volume accumulator that attempts to improve on the on-balance volume indicator. One problem with OBV is that the entire volume is assigned to a given day regardless of intraday price movement.

Chaikin uses a different approach. He calculates the day's closing price as a percentage of the day's range and assigns that percentage of the volume to the accumulator. Thus, if the market closed up and the price ranged from 300 to 305 but closed at 303, Chaikin would add 60 percent of the total daily volume to the previous day's total. If the market closed down and the market ranged from 300 to 295 but closed at 296, he would subtract 80 percent of the total daily volume from the previous day's total. His formula is:

$$\text{Adjusted volume} = ((C - L) - (H - C)) \div (H - L) \times V$$

Chaikin's volume accumulator should work best in oscillating markets rather than in trending markets.

John Murphy suggests constructing a three-day and a ten-day moving average and then plotting the difference between the two as a histogram. As with MACD and the MACD histogram, you then can draw trendlines, look for crossovers between the two moving averages, look for penetration of the zero line by both averages and look for the volume histogram to cross the zero line. You also can look for divergences between the price trend and volume accumulation. This approach may suggest underlying patterns of accumulation and distribution in the market.

The volume accumulator is best used in essentially trendless or sideways markets with low directional movement, whereas on-balance volume is better suited for strongly trending markets. Chaikin's oscillator should prove extremely useful in the same situations where stochastics work the best.

VOLUME PERCENTAGE RATIO

Another approach that is particularly useful when the market has a strong trend is the volume percentage ratio. Subtract down volume from up volume and then divide the remainder by total volume—on a daily basis. You then construct a ten-day simple moving average and compare that line to price movement. Again, you look for confirmation or divergence.

The volume percentage ratio avoids one major problem associated with volume indicators. Most volume-based indicators have a built-in upward bias because they are based on total volume. On days in which the market is up, total volume is likely to be large. Thus, the difference between up and down volume is likely to be relatively greater than on days in which prices decline and total volume is low. (This is the converse of the long-term advance minus decline line, which has a built-in negative bias.) Because the market has an upside bias and because volume indicators also have an upside bias, this may explain why many analysts think that volume indicators are leading indicators.

UP MINUS DOWN VOLUME

The simplest method for the average investor is to create a 10-day, 50-day or 200-day up minus down volume indicator. In each case, you subtract the total down volume from the total up volume for each day and average the data over the desired length of time. You then compare the trend in volume to the trend in the daily closing prices of the DJIA, looking for confirmation or nonconfirmation of the price trend.

Unfortunately, for each stock, whether volume is labeled up or down for the day is determined by the price of the last trade for the day. Thus, if the previous day's last trade on stock XYZ had been 50.25 and today's last trade was 50.50, all the volume for today would be up volume. Because the majority of the day's trading might have been below 50.25, the emphasis on the last trade injects a large element of noise into the statistics for any single stock or index. This is another reason why you must look for confirmation from a variety of indicators.

RICHARD ARMS'S EASE-OF-MOVEMENT
INDICATOR

A number of more sophisticated approaches to volume analysis have been developed by market technicians. Most of these approaches have been designed for very specific purposes and can be used to supplement the information obtained from other, more traditional volume indicators.

Richard Arms has developed an ease-of-movement indicator that attempts to measure market elasticity.[16] To calculate his indicator, you subtract yesterday's median price from today's median price. You then divide the difference by today's volume divided by today's range. You then construct a 13-day simple moving average of the indicator and plot a zero line. When the SMA crosses above the zero line, it is a buy signal. When it crosses below the zero line, it is a sell signal.

While it is hard to establish target zones for the daily data, large spikes downward in the daily ease-of-movement indicator often coincide with the ends of rallies (or declines). If the daily bar charts provide evidence of a reversal pattern at the same time that the ease-of-movement indicator spikes downward, you have a much better chance of identifying the end of the current short-term trend. A move that begins on a fairly large upward spike in the daily ease-of-movement indicator often requires an equally large spike downward in the daily indicator before the move is over. There is no obvious explanation for this phenomenon and it is only a rough rule of thumb.

ACCUMULATION AND DISTRIBUTION

Many analysts attempt to identify patterns of accumulation and distribution. (Sometimes this approach is called money-flow analysis.) According to technical analysts, smart money anticipates major moves in the market and sees value in specific stocks long before the rest of the herd perceives these values. Thus, smart money begins to buy stocks (accumulation) while the price still is relatively low. Similarly, smart money perceives a top in the stock (or market) long before the common mass of humanity and begins to sell the stock (distribution) before other investors begin unloading that stock.

Indicators such as the negative volume index are designed to reveal price action on days when volume is declining. Supposedly, light volume days are days in which public participation is less and professional buying and selling is relatively more significant. There are, however, some theoretical problems with this indicator. Specifically, because a strong positive correlation between volume and prices exists, you would expect this indicator to have a long-term negative bias.

A more promising method of studying money flow is to calculate the volume of shares multiplied by the price of the stock (or index) on an uptick and subtract the volume multiplied by the price of shares on a downtick.[17] That cumulative line then is compared to the closing prices of that stock or index.[18] Eighty percent of the time, the money-flow line parallels the price trend. When divergences occur, however, this usually is a sign of a likely change in the stock or index in the direction indicated by the money-flow line. This is one of the more promising refinements in the field of volume analysis. Unfortunately, such data is both difficult and expensive to obtain; generally, technical analysts must subscribe to a special service to receive this information.

FIRST HOUR MINUS LAST HOUR INDICATOR

A simple method of studying the broader market is suggested by Lynn Elgert who calculates the difference between the last hour of trading and the first hour of trading.[19] In theory, if you subtract the change in prices for the first hour of trading from the change in prices during the last hour of trading, you get an indication of the difference between smart money and not-so-smart money. Supposedly, those who trade in the first hour of the day include foreigners and small investors who receive their reports in summary form at the end of the trading day and then issue buy or sell orders to be executed on the opening. Very different are the last-hour traders who tend to be professionals who can afford to spend the day analyzing price trends and are able to step into the market to buy or sell during the last hour of the trading session, i.e., 3:00 to 4:00 P.M. (EST).

A further refinement might be to take the first and last half-hour of the trading day under the theory that overnight and early morning orders are executed on the open and that professionals wait until after the bond market closes to make their final decisions of the day. In any case, the philosophy of the smart money-flow indicator is similar to the negative volume and positive volume indicators, although the calculations are entirely different. In each case, the technician attempts to identify what professionals and amateurs are doing, with the assumption that when the two disagree, the professionals are more likely to be correct.

VOLUME AS A SENTIMENT INDICATOR

According to Jim Yates, about 90 percent of the volume on the NYSE is the result of institutional trading.[20] Because institutions have a reputation for poor market timing, high volume on the NYSE should be associated with market tops and market bottoms. A 20-day moving average of volume along with standard deviation bands works fairly well as a market-timing indicator.

ARMS INDEX

Developed by Richard Arms, the Arms index, also known as the TRIN, or Trading index, is widely followed by technical analysts as an overbought/oversold indicator.[21] The Arms index combines advance/decline data with volume data. The number of shares advancing for each day is divided by the number of shares declining on the NYSE. Then, volume up is divided by volume down. The first ratio then is divided by the second to create the index. Ten days of index readings are averaged to give the ten-day index. Supposedly, a reading over 1.20 is extremely oversold, while a reading of below 0.80 is extremely overbought.

The Arms index focuses attention on buying volume versus selling volume. Too much volume in too few stocks suggests that the rally (or sell-off) is unlikely to be sustained. By contrast, a more normal ratio between volume in advancing stocks and volume in declining stocks suggests a market that already is in dynamic equilibrium.

Bollinger suggests that the long-term bias of the market is upward and, therefore, the long-term average of the ten-day Arms index is closer to 0.85 than to 1.00.[22] In bull markets, when the ten-day ARMS index reaches 0.65 or lower, the market is seriously overbought on a **short-term** basis. When it reaches 1.10 or higher, it is seriously oversold. At such levels, the market is likely to correct in the opposite direction.

Bollinger also suggests treating the Arms index in much the same way as you might treat the McClellan oscillator (which was discussed previously). Thus, you look for severe overbought or oversold conditions at the start of a major rally. You look for confirmation in the up/down volume ratio. You assume that the subsequent readings of the Arms index will continue to be overbought (or oversold) but at a more modest level.

It also is extremely useful to look at the relative change in stock prices and compare that to the daily Arms index. In other words, you are looking at the amount of buying (or selling) pressure required to move the market to some specified level or amount. If the index reading is extremely low yet the stock market rallies only slightly, this suggests that there is considerable overhead resistance. If the index reading is extremely high yet the market decline is relatively small, this suggests that there is considerable support at that level. What is more ominous is a market decline where the daily Arms index is below 1.0, i.e., the market supposedly was overbought that day. This may suggest that conditions are right for a continued sell-off. Used with some care, the Arms index is a powerful tool for stock-market analysis.

John Bollinger correctly points out that ratios can be misinterpreted by the unwary for they provide a geometric, not an arithmetic, distribution.[23] Thus, a reading of 0.50 is as overbought as a reading of 2.00 is oversold. In addition, there are problems associated with using the Arms index for periods greater than one day. Bollinger points out that if you average two readings that are equally intense, e.g., 0.50 and 2.00, you will get 1.25 rather than the correct answer of 1.00.[24] He suggests calculating the ten-day Open Arms index to create an indicator that is easier to interpret. To calculate the Open Arms index, you average each of the components and then calculate the appropriate ratio, e.g., 10 days or 50 days.

JERRY FAVORS'S TREND FIVE

Jerry Favors is an Elliott Wave theorist who has developed a variation on the Arms index that may have some merit. Favors adds the past five days of closing Arms index readings in a five-day moving sum he calls the Trend Five. If that sum reaches six or more, it is a sign of a market bottom. If it reaches four or less, it is a sign of a market top.

HERRICK PAYOFF INDEX (HPI)

The Herrick Payoff Index (HPI) is an attempt to combine open interest, volume and price action. Used with futures contracts, this is a form of money-flow indicator. You look for negative divergence between price action and the HPI. The HPI is calculated as follows: Add to yesterday's HPI (K_y) K^1 minus K_y multiplied by S (a smoothing factor, e.g., 0.1). Divide that number by 100,000.

$$\text{HPI} = \frac{K_y + [(K^1 - K_y)S]}{100,000}$$

$K^1 = [(M - M_y) \times C \times V] \times [I + \text{or} - (I \times 2/6)]$, where y is yesterday's value; M is the mean price,[25] or high minus low, divided by 2; C is the value of a \$0.01 move; V is the volume; and I is the absolute value of today's open interest minus yesterday's open interest.

One disadvantage of the Herrick Payoff Index is that open interest figures are released one day late. For the day-trader, the HPI is not useful. For someone with a longer time horizon, however, the HPI is very useful. In any case, if you use the Herrick Payoff Index, be careful not to use either the RSI:14 (daily) or the Demand index for confirmation. These three indicators provide much the same information and should be regarded as redundant.

Endnotes

1. Interview with John Bollinger, FNN, 11 April 1989.

2. In response to a question posed by Liebe Geft on "Shop Talk," FNN, 28 September 1989.

3. *The Richland Report,* #88–9 (7 May 1988).

4. Interview with Diana Koricke, FNN, 20 March 1989.

5. "Count Down," FNN, 17 July 1989.

6. "Count Down," interview with Gary Salem, FNN, 3 July 1989.

7. "Guru Review," with Jeff Bower, FNN, 5 October 1990.

8. "Count Down," interview with Diana Koricke, FNN, 8 May 1989.

9. Interview with Diana Koricke, FNN, 13 February 1989.

10. FNN, 21 November 1988.

11. Interview with Ron Insana, FNN, 7 November 1988.

12. "The Donoghue Strategies," interview with Bill Donoghue, FNN, 18 August 1989.

13. "Wall Street Week," with Louis Rukeyser, 4 May 1990.

14. Thomas Aspray, "Using volume and open interest to confirm price trend directions," *Futures* (April 1989): 38–40.

15. "Shop Talk," FNN, 28 November 1989.

16. See *Technical Analysis of Stocks and Commodities,* vol. 8, no. 5 (May 1990): 52–56.

17. This information is available for home computers through the Knight-Ridder Trade Center service.

18. As explained by Simon Langdon, Yield Pack Equity Services, Knight-Ridder Trade Center, New York, during an interview with John Bollinger, FNN, 23 November 1988.

19. "Wall Street Week," 9 December 1988.

20. "The Options Report," interview with Bill Griffeth, FNN, 30 May 1989.

21. Richard Arms, *The Arms Index* (Homewood, Ill.: Dow Jones-Irwin, 1989).

22. "Count Down," FNN, 30 March 1989.

23. "Investment Monograph: The Arms Index," *John Bollinger's Capital Growth Letter* (May 1991).

24. Ibid.

25. While some standard texts on technical analysis call this the mean price, it actually is the midpoint.

9

Reading the Tea Leaves: Some Indirect Evidence

While breadth, volume and leadership indicators are very useful for the confirmation of or nonconfirmation of price trends, there are a great variety of ways market analysts find indirect evidence of the health of the general market. Some of these systems have remarkable track records.

MARKET BELLWETHERS

One of the simplest systems to predict the future course of the stock market is to watch the behavior of market bellwethers such as IBM and General Motors. Because these stocks represent a very large percentage of the total capitalization of the S&P 500, some analysts have suggested that these two stocks indicate where the broader stock market might be headed. When these stocks head upward but the market lags, this supposedly is an encouraging sign, i.e., a positive divergence. When these two stocks head lower but the market continues to rally, however, this supposedly is a negative sign, i.e., a negative divergence.

As Figure 9.1 indicates, IBM reached a peak in the August–September period of 1989, before the 13 October 1989 minicrash. It then sold off abruptly in October and continued its down trend into early January while the DJIA reached postcrash highs at the same time. At that point, the Dow sold off abruptly, which was something that had been foreshadowed by the behavior of both IBM and General Motors (see Figure 9.2).

FIGURE 9.1   IBM, May 1989 to February 1990

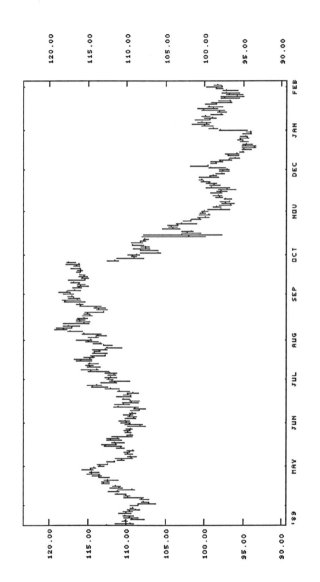

Robert Stovall is one technician who has continued to watch General Motors and follow its performance as a market bellwether. Stovall claims that any failure of General Motors to make a new high within four months of a previous high is a warning of the end of the current bull market and a possible market decline ahead. Similarly, if General Motors fails to make a new market low within four months of a previous low, this is a sign of the end of a current bear market and a market rally ahead. Stovall claims that the General Motors bellwether has been right about 70 percent of the time.

Analysts often claim that one or another of these two traditional bellwethers has lost its value. Be suspicious of such claims. While either of these two bellwethers might fail on occasion, taken together, these two stocks provide very useful information. When both stocks are rallying, they confirm a rally in the broader market averages. When both stocks are declining, they confirm a sell-off in the broader averages. When these two stocks evidence bullish or bearish divergences from the rest of the market, however, an important early warning signal is generated.

UTILITY STOCKS AND INTEREST RATES

Many analysts claim that utility prices predict the course of interest rates. This is a fallacy. Utility prices reveal what conservative investors assume is the probable direction of interest rates and the economy. A safe haven in times of recession—along with food and drug stocks—utility companies traditionally have been quite interest-sensitive. Thus, if investors think that interest rates have peaked, they may want to invest in utility stocks. Quite often, these investors are correct—but not always.

A more serious problem is created by the fact that most analysts follow the Dow Jones list of 15 utilities. Because the performance of only two or three of these stocks can have a significant impact on the performance of the average, it would be wiser to follow the NYSE list of utility stocks that represents a much broader list. Nevertheless, the Dow Jones Utility Index continues to serve as an excellent bellwether for both the DJIA and the S&P 500. John Murphy claims that the Dow utilities "have a tremendous record for leading the industrials, at tops in particular."[1]

FIGURE 9.2   General Motors, April 1989 to February 1990

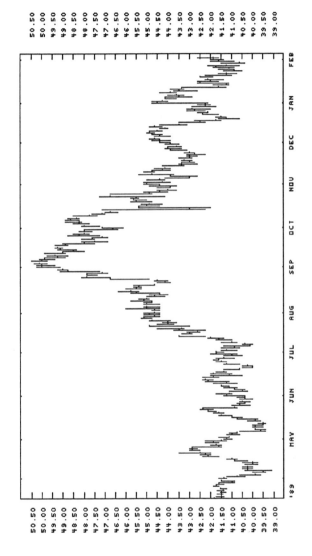

BANK STOCKS AND REAL ESTATE PRICES

During the real estate and savings and loan crises of 1989–1990, the prices of bank stocks dropped precipitously—before most people became aware of the problems of the thrift and banking industries in their areas. This simply is because investors in thrift and banking stocks are very aware of changes in the amount of nonperforming loans. A rise in nonperforming loans usually precedes any foreclosures and thus is likely to be reflected in the price of bank stocks long before the general public is fully aware of the situation.

The stock market is likely to be healthy when both the utility stocks and the financial stocks (banks, brokerages and insurance companies) are in a bullish up trend. Similarly, the stock market is likely to be dangerous when utility and financial stocks are in a down trend.

COMMODITY STOCKS AND COMMODITY PRICES

The stocks of companies that produce or process commodities often anticipate changes in the price of the underlying commodity. Gold stocks, for example, usually anticipate changes in the price of gold bullion, just as oil company stocks usually anticipate changes in the price of crude oil. Look for the price of the stocks to confirm the trend of the commodities. When there are divergences, however, bet on the stocks to be leading indicators. This works so well and so often that it is one of the more reliable bellwethers to follow.

Since 1987, the price of gold bullion seems to have been inversely proportional to the price of the S&P 500. (See Figure 9.3 for an illustration of this relationship in 1989.) This suggests that a diversified gold stock mutual fund might be an appropriate trading vehicle for a no-load mutual fund investor who might be looking for a synthetic short. (A short is selling a stock that you do not own.)

When you get a sell signal from your timing model, you want, in theory, to close out your long positions and go short. The problem for most no-load mutual fund investors is that the great majority of mutual funds does not offer that possibility. Buying a gold stock mutual fund offers the prospect of some capital appreciation while the general market is headed lower.

FIGURE 9.3 Gold Prices versus DJIA, January 1989 to January 1990

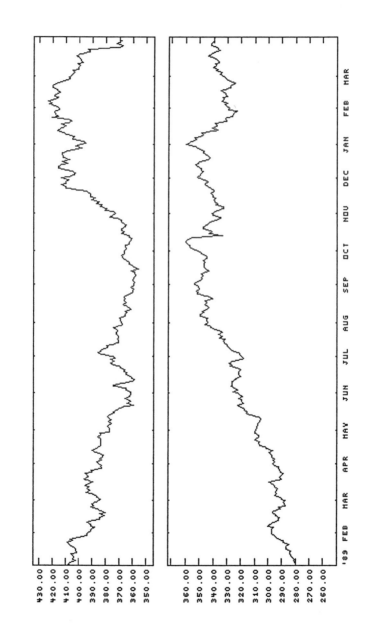

Whether gold is a good inflation hedge depends on a variety of factors. Only when the market is convinced that inflation is a problem does gold seem to move strongly. Ed Hart of CNBC/FNN suggests that it takes a combination of fear of inflation along with negative real interest rates on Treasury bonds to encourage investors to purchase gold.[2] An alternative conceptual framework is provided by Edward Cousins who believes that U.S. monetary growth is strongly correlated with the price of gold. Thus, a rapidly growing money supply puts upward pressure on gold prices, while a contracting money supply puts downward pressure on the price of gold.

Steven Nison suggests that a 40-week moving average has proven to be extremely useful for gold traders. He also says that gold retracements tend to be 50 percent of the major move. Since 1982, gold has had a trading range from a low of $300 to a high of $500 per ounce.

TEMPORARY EMPLOYEES

Look at the price of stocks of companies that provide temporary personnel as a potential leading economic indicator for the broader market and economy. Many firms hire temporaries because of special corporate needs unrelated to the economy. But as large numbers of companies experience a sudden increase in order flow, they are likely to hire temporaries to reduce the risk of future layoffs and of having to pay unemployment compensation and other benefits. Thus, at the end of a long recession, companies may prefer the flexibility that comes with hiring temporary personnel. As the economy begins to decline, the temporary employees are the first to be let go. In that case, the stocks of those companies should reflect rather accurately any changes in business activity.

CURRENCY MARKETS

International demand for stocks, bonds and commodities is directly affected by the currency markets. A declining dollar eventually makes all American commodities, including manufactured goods, agricultural products, stocks, bonds and real estate, relatively more attractive to buyers. As long as the dollar is falling, however, foreign buyers will be likely to delay their purchases of American stocks and bonds to avoid capital loss. But after the dollar has bottomed out, foreign buyers may see an opportunity for additional capital appreciation because of a rising dollar. Thus, any perception that a decline in the dollar is about to reverse itself is especially bullish. Similarly, any perception that a rising dollar is about to reverse direction is particularly bearish.

The value of the dollar can have a powerful effect on stock prices. Martin Zweig points out that a long-term decline in the dollar from 1971 to 1980 was accompanied by a long-term bear market for stocks, with about a two-year lag.[3] When the dollar rallied from 1980 to 1985, the stock market also rallied, again with a two-year lag. The peak in the dollar late in 1985 presaged a peak in the stock market some two years later. While the trend in the value of the dollar is not always useful for short-term timing purposes, it, nevertheless, is useful for a general assessment of investment risks and opportunities over several months' time.

OTHER MARKETS

John Murphy is the foremost exponent of intermarket analysis. Murphy recommends that you look at a variety of markets to confirm or deny impressions of the current trend in the stock market. Look first at the U.S. dollar as measured by the dollar index. A declining dollar tends to be bullish for commodity prices, while a rising dollar usually is bearish. Next, look at the behavior of the CRB futures index. This is a list of 21 commodities with heavy emphasis on agricultural commodities. Commodity prices should move in a direction opposite to bond prices. According to Murphy, the bond and commodities markets (CRB) have the closest relationship of all the various markets. When commodity prices are rising, the bond market should be falling and vice versa. A rising bond market usually is bullish for stock prices, while a declining bond market usually is bearish for stocks. While the stock and bond markets tend to move in tandem, the bond market sometimes leads the stock market.

NEWS

If an investor watches the market's reaction to news events, he or she can gain valuable short-term insight into market psychology. A market that goes up on good news and down on bad news is neutral. A market that goes up on bad news is very bullish. A market that goes down on good news is very bearish. These rules seem to have the benefit of common sense behind them. The problem is that there are all types of news that might affect the markets. At times, the markets shrug off a bad report, and at other times, the markets react strongly.

An excellent example of market reaction to news is the response of the market after the release of merchandise trade deficit figures on 10 December 1987. The statistics for October were much worse than expected. The market fell 57 points (or 3 percent) on that news on the 10th. The dollar made new lows versus the yen for the next three days. But the stock market rallied 150 points (or 8 percent) over the next nine days and broke above the upper line of a triangle formation.

For several months late in 1986, the markets seemed concerned with money supply data. In 1987, the dollar seemed to preoccupy many analysts. In 1988, the new enthusiasm was interest rates. The greatest value of watching market reaction to news is that you get a sense of the bullishness of the actual players in the market as opposed to the so-called experts.

Perhaps the simplest way to proceed is to watch how the market reacts to unexpected events that financial commentators regard as bullish (or bearish). If the market rises (or declines) on such news, the market is behaving normally. If, however, the market sells off on bullish news, that can be extremely bearish. Conversely, if the market rallies on supposedly bearish news, that can be extremely bullish. Look, in particular, at the market's reaction to unexpected changes in interest rates, employment data, inflation reports and trade deficits.

Endnotes

1. CNBC/FNN, 12 June 1991.
2. "Market Wrap," FNN, 18 November 1988.
3. *The Zweig Forecast*, 18 November 1988.
4. Interview with Bill Griffeth, FNN, 14 October 1988.

10

An Eclectic Approach

To develop some perspective on the financial markets, you must look at a variety of indicators, including valuation, money supply, interest rates, market behavior, sentiment, breadth, volume and leadership. The following list is intended as a summary of the indicators worth following on a daily or weekly basis.

Weekly

Valuation:

1. Price-dividend ratio
2. Estimated equilibrium price minus actual price
3. Price-to-book ratio
4. Price-earnings ratio

Economic:

5. GDP
6. Unemployment rate
7. Employment growth
8. Consumer Price Index
9. Leading indicators composite index
10. Real retail sales
11. Nondefense durable goods orders
12. New housing starts
13. Producer Price Index for crude goods
14. Merchandise trade deficit

15. Current accounts deficit
16. Consumer installment debt
17. Capacity utilization
18. Unit labor costs

Monetary:

19. Growth of real M3
20. Net-free reserves
21. Norman Fosback's mutual fund cash position indicator

Interest Rates:

22. Three-month Treasury-bill rates
23. Federal funds rate
24. Discount rate
25. 30-year Treasury-bond rate

Sentiment:

26. Ansbacher index
27. AAII bullish percentage divided by bulls plus bears
28. Market Vane bullishness
29. *Investor's Intelligence* bulls minus bears
30. Sales-redemption ratio of mutual funds

Daily

Price:

31. ADXR
32. MACD
33. 20-day moving average with volatility bands
34. 13-week moving average with volatility bands
35. RSI:14 (daily and weekly) with a nine-day SMA of itself

Advances and Declines:

36. Ten-day advance minus decline line
37. McClellan oscillator

38. Cumulative advance minus decline line

Volume:

39. Ten-day volume percentage ratio
40. On-balance volume indicator
41. Ten-day up minus down volume
42. Ten-day Open Arms

Highs and Lows:

43. Five-day moving average of new highs minus new lows
44. 20-day moving average of new highs minus new lows

TIME HORIZONS OF MARKET INDICATORS

Most novice technical analysts find it difficult to identify the appropriate time horizons for their indicators. The longer the moving average used in the calculations, the longer the lag between market action and indicator signals. Value and economic indicators are particularly useful to gain some assessment of the longer-term outlook for the market, while internal market indicators tend to reflect short-term phenomena. Monetary indicators seem to be valuable for an intermediate-term outlook.

TARGET PRICES AND THE SWING RULE

Target prices for a rally or a decline can be identified in many ways. A combination of targets derived from three different systems is likely to prove more useful than targets based on just one system.

Support and resistance levels are the most common method, especially for markets in a trading range. For markets with a strong trend, short-term targets can be established using the upper and lower bands of trend channels.

Bollinger bands also can be used to provide targets for market moves based on volatility. When a market is at the lower band, the first target is the moving average, while the secondary target is the upper band. Likewise, when the market is at the upper band, the first target to the downside is the moving average, while the secondary target is the lower band.

A third set of short-term target prices is provided by Stan Weinstein's swing rule. You measure the distance between a market peak and the nearest support level. When the market violates that support level, it suggests a downward target of approximately the same distance below the support level. Similarly, if you measure the distance between a market bottom and the nearest resistance level, when the market penetrates that resistance level, the swing rule suggests an upside target of approximately that distance above the resistance level.

SYSTEMATIC MARKET ANALYSIS

Begin your analysis of the stock market with a series of questions: Is the market overvalued, undervalued or properly priced? Are investors generally optimistic or pessimistic? Is the public heavily involved in the stock market? Has the dollar been trending upward or downward over the past two years? Has real M3 been increasing or decreasing? At a constant or accelerating rate? Are short-term interest rates increasing or decreasing? How rapidly? What is happening to the yields on the 30-year Treasury bond? Is the yield curve positively or negatively sloped? Is the Treasury-bill yield above or below the discount rate? Are federal funds rates trending lower or higher? Has the Fed been intervening in the market at intervention time? With customer or system repurchases? How large are net-free reserves? Are they increasing or decreasing? Is the mutual fund cash indicator bullish or bearish? These questions are fundamental and identify the general investment climate. Thus, they should precede any other analysis.

Next, look at stock-market indicators. How do the current price-dividend and price-earnings ratios compare to historic benchmarks? Is the market in a trending or oscillating mode? Over the past several months, has the cumulative advance minus decline line been rising or falling? What about the cumulative new highs minus new lows line? Does the cumulative up minus down volume line confirm the longer-term trend? This analysis will give you a good idea of the longer-term prospects for the market.

Next, look at the ten-day moving average of advances minus declines, the ten-day moving average of up minus down volume and the five-day moving average of new highs minus new lows. Do these indicators confirm the price movement of the market over the past 20 days? Remember that short-term indicators lead the intermediate-term indicators, which then lead the longer-term indicators at important market turning points.

Look, especially, at the 20-day, 65-day and 200-day moving averages of the DJIA along with their volatility bands. These moving averages will give you a good idea of the short-term, intermediate-term and long-term trends in the market as well as how overbought or oversold the market may be in each of these three time frames. Is the market above (or below) important support (or resistance) extending back several months or more? Do price momentum indicators such as RSI:14 confirm the current trend?

Based on your timing model, identify whether the odds favor a rally or a decline over the next few weeks or months. Then, identify stop-loss points where you would exit the market if your timing model generates a losing trade.

BUY AND SELL CHECKLISTS

For those who are less mathematically or visually inclined, an impressionistic approach to stock-market timing may prove useful. Richard Crowell developed a Time-To-Buy checklist and a Time-To-Sell checklist that were revised by Charles Rolo. Review these checklists once a month. Answer questions with "yes," "no" or "uncertain." When you have a great preponderance of "yes" answers on the sell checklist, you should anticipate a weak market ahead. When you have a great preponderance of "yes" answers on the buy checklist, you should anticipate a strong market ahead.

Crowell's Time-To-Buy Checklist[1]

1. Is business activity nationally in a down trend, and if so, do you foresee the end to that down trend?

2. Is inflation decelerating?
3. Have corporate profits declined from their previous peak, and if so, do you expect them to start upward soon?
4. Is the economic news largely negative and are most forecasters pessimistic?
5. Have short-term interest rates started to decline?
6. Has the Federal Reserve Board given indications that there will be an easing of monetary policy?
7. What is the P/E ratio of the S&P index or the DJIA? Is it approaching or below the P/E ratio at the last cyclical low point of the market?
8. Are the mutual funds heavily in cash?
9. Is the odd-lot short-sales ratio exceptionally high?
10. Is the specialists' short-sales ratio exceptionally low?
11. Are your friends and business associates pessimistic or apathetic about the market?
12. Has the market been declining for many months since its previous cyclical high?
13. Has the market registered a large drop from its previous cyclical high?
14. Has the market recently accelerated its rate of decline, which is typical of the final stages of bear markets?
15. Does the market appear to have bottomed? Has it rebounded from its low point, tested that low several times without falling below it and then started to advance?

Crowell's Time-To-Sell Checklist[2]

1. Is there growing evidence of a business-cycle peak?
2. Is inflation accelerating?
3. Has the rate of gain of corporate profits slowed or is the current rate too strong to last?
4. Are most of the economic forecasts optimistic?
5. Are short-term interest rates rising and are they as high as they were at the corresponding stage of the previous business upturn?
6. Has the Federal Reserve Board started to tighten monetary policy?

7. What is the market's P/E ratio? Has it approached or risen above the P/E at the last cyclical peak of the market?
8. Are the cash reserves of the mutual funds low?
9. Is the odd-lot short-sales ratio exceptionally low?
10. Is the specialists' short-sales ratio exceptionally high?
11. Are your friends and business associates talking about winners they've bought and feeling euphoric about the market?
12. Has the market been advancing for many months since its previous cyclical low?
13. Has the market registered a large percentage gain from its previous cyclical low?
14. Is the advance/decline line underperforming the popular averages?
15. Does the market appear to have peaked? Has the Dow dropped below its recent high and climbed back to it a couple of times or more, but only to retreat again?

These checklists are useful, but you should not follow them slavishly. They are intended for the purpose of general market orientation and are not a substitute for a more precise market-timing model.

IDENTIFYING MARKET TOPS AND BOTTOMS

Analysts claim that it is much harder to identify a major market top than to identify a major market bottom. You might use the following criteria to alert you to the possibility that the market may be on the verge of a major trend change.

After a long rally that takes the market up at least 25 percent (and preferably 50 to 75 percent) from a major market bottom, look for market valuations to be getting expensive, e.g., the market P/E to be 20 to 1 or higher, the price-dividend ratio to be 33 to 1 or higher and the price-to-book ratio to be 2.5 to 1 or higher. Near most major market tops, short-term interest rates may be rising. Sentiment should be excessively bullish as measured by a variety of indicators, including futures traders' sentiment, advisory sentiment, the put-call ratio and institutional cash. Corporate insiders are likely to be selling stocks in their companies. Look for commercial traders to be net short. Watch for the Dow Jones Utilities Index to break recent support. Look for a decline of 80+ percent in the number of daily new highs. RSI:14 (weekly) may be diverging negatively from the price series. Remember, these are simply guidelines, not iron laws of technical analysis. When the market violates an upwardly sloping line of support connecting the lowest intraday lows of at least two countertrend sell-off bottoms, you may be very close to the start of a major sell-off. Draw that line so that it connects the first reaction low to the reaction low immediately preceding the peak, provided that this line does not intersect any daily price bars.

To identify a major market bottom, look for prices to have declined at least 20 percent from a recent high. In most cases, short-term interest rates should be declining. Sentiment should be excessively bearish. Corporate insiders should be buying stocks in their own companies. Look for commercial traders to be net long. The DJUI may be breaking above recent highs. Look for a shrinkage of new lows. Watch also for a bullish divergence on RSI:14 (weekly). Again, these are simply guidelines. One or more of these indicators may not be flashing a warning signal. When the market violates a downwardly sloping line of resistance connecting at least two countertrend rally tops, you may be very close to the start of a major rally. To draw that line correctly, connect the top of the first reaction high to the top of the reaction high immediately preceding the bottom, provided that this line does not intersect any daily price bars.

Endnotes

1. Adapted from Richard A. Crowell, *Stock Market Strategy* (New York: McGraw-Hill, 1977), p. 105. © 1983 by Richard A. Crowell.
2. Ibid.

11

Trading Systems

A huge difference exists between the ability to analyze the market and the ability to trade it successfully. Many of the market-timing systems developed by market technicians work extremely well. Every system, however, has the potential for occasional failure. If you are going to beat the broader market averages, you must know what to do when your favorite indicator or timing model fails. For example, what do you do if your model has just given a sell signal and then the market suddenly takes off in a huge rally? Alternatively, what do you do if your model has just given a buy signal but the market plummets?

Bruce Babcock has published a superb guide to trading systems that should be required reading for every investor and stock-market trader.[1] Babcock argues that futures and commodities markets are traded in the same way, that fundamental analysis is less profitable than technical trading systems, that a purely mechanical trading system will prove superior to those based on hunch or intuition, that ego drives most traders and that some losses are inevitable. Babcock's three basic principles are: Follow the trend, cut your losses short and let your profits ride. Because futures commissions typically are 5 percent of the charges for similar stock purchases, leverage is much higher. Thus, potential profits and losses are much higher. Babcock insists that the trader must follow a disciplined trading strategy and never bet more than he or she can afford to lose. Babcock warns the trader to watch for slippage (the difference between the price at the time you decide to buy or sell and the price at which you actually buy or sell) and the bid-ask spread that causes the trader always to buy at the higher ask price and always to sell at the lower bid price.

Babcock says that some people are more comfortable with day trading, while others have longer time horizons. He suggests trading the time frame with which you are most comfortable. He cautions against taking profits too soon. He says that you can't predict the market, so don't try. You should have realistic expectations. Just try to break even the first year, to make 20 percent the second year and 50 percent every year from then on. Babcock counsels being patient. Wait for the right opportunity to trade your system. Don't chase the market. If the market takes off without you, wait for a pullback or don't trade that move.

Babcock warns the reader about various con games, including supposedly surefire systems. Don't look for a perfect system because none exists. Systems that are curve-fit or excessively optimized may generate tremendous trades against historical data but will not necessarily work in the future. Random reinforcement makes learning how to trade more difficult as even some of your mistakes turn out to be profitable.

You must develop a system that produces a good percentage of winning trades, but Babcock says that a very high percentage of winning trades may be the result of small winners and larger losers. He says that professional traders do not mind using a system that might produce just 40 percent winners—if the winners are large and the losers are small. Cumulative profit-or-loss statistics are useful but can be misleading. If the profit margin per trade is small, then the system can produce large total profits with very little margin for error. A good trading system has a high ratio of average win to average loss (at least two to one), "depending on the percentage of profitable trades."[2] As Babcock explains, "the profit factor is the ratio of the total net profit from profitable trades divided by the total net profit from losing trades: a break-even system has a profit factor of one."[3] If you look at the average trading length of winning and losing trades, you get some idea not only of whether the system is a long-term or short-term trading system but also whether the system cuts losses short and lets profits ride.

FOUR-WEEK RULE

One simple example of a trading system is the four-week rule. John Murphy recommends using four weeks of price data as a filter to prevent being whipsawed in trendless or sideways markets. The rule is quite simple. You close out shorts and go long whenever the current price is above the highest close for the past four weeks. You close out long positions and go short whenever the current price is below the lowest close of the previous four weeks. With the four-week rule, you require a breakout before trading. Thus, the four-week rule is both a trading system and a stop-loss system.

In strongly trending markets, the four-week rule can be modified so that you initiate long positions when prices are above the highest close for the previous four weeks, but then you close out those long positions any time you close below the lowest close of the previous two weeks. Similarly, you go short whenever you close below the lowest close of the previous four weeks, but you close out those shorts whenever the price rises above the highest close for the previous two weeks. If you use this modification, be careful. In trendless markets, this system is likely to lead to a series of whipsaws.

DANGER OF REDUNDANCY

Many market indicators duplicate one another. If you make the mistake of building a model that comprises several redundant indicators, you will receive impressive R-square readings on regression tests but you may not be improving the real accuracy of your model. A much better approach would be to find three or four indicators that you understand well and that are not highly intercorrelated. Pay close attention to whether these indicators are used for short-term, intermediate-term or long-term timing. Find the time horizon that best suits your own personality. Then, see if you can put them together into something that works well against historical data. These principles are implicit in the six market-timing systems that are described on the following pages.

SIX EXAMPLES OF INTERMEDIATE-TERM
TIMING SYSTEMS

My own market-timing model, described in Chapter 12, is based on sentiment as a contrary indicator and works extremely well. That model requires the investor to buy when the experts are advising you to sell and to sell when the experts are advising you to buy. For that reason, many small investors may not have the discipline to follow it faithfully.

A variety of alternative approaches to market timing exists, however, and these approaches should fit different personalities and learning styles. This chapter contains six examples of intermediate-term market-timing systems that approach the subject from very different theoretical perspectives. Each has its own strengths and weaknesses. They are intended for an active, aggressive investor who enjoys technical analysis and is willing to spend some time working with data to develop and test his or her own system. These six models are not intended for the type of person who would be more comfortable following a buy-and-hold strategy, the recommendations of a professional market newsletter or the signals of a commercial market-timing model.

If you are the type of person who likes to experiment with timing models and make your own independent decisions, perhaps one of these approaches will stimulate your own thinking. To use these models, you must gather and analyze some historical data using either a spreadsheet or one of several technical analysis programs intended for the personal computer.

The six models described on the following pages are intended as starting points in your own analysis. Each has the potential to become the cornerstone of a larger, more sophisticated market-timing model. All six models have the potential to capture significant moves in the stock market that take a few weeks to a few months to accomplish. All are intended for no-load mutual funds, especially those indexed to major market averages. For each model, you must record the daily high, low, opening and closing price of the index you wish to trade, along with the total volume of shares traded on that index each day. Follow four major averages for which such data is readily available in most newspapers: the DJIA, the S&P 500, the NASDAQ and the

NYSE. These models should work with all four indexes because they are highly intercorrelated in terms of price swings up or down. Naturally, to make the most money, you want to use the index that is showing the greatest relative strength, i.e., is rising the fastest on up days and declining the least on down days.

TREND-FOLLOWING SYSTEM

If you are most comfortable with a trend-following system, consider Welles Wilder's Directional Oscillator (DIOSC). (The DIOSC is composed of a 14-day average of the +DI minus a 14-day average of the -DI.) If the market is in an up trend as defined by point-and-figure charts, go long on buy signals and to cash on sell signals. If the market is in a down trend, go short on sell signals and cover your shorts and go to cash on buy signals. When the DIOSC rises above the zero line, you have a buy signal. When the DIOSC falls below the zero line, you have a sell signal. Note divergences between the chart of the DIOSC and the chart of the index to warn you of momentum failure. Treat these divergences as early warning signs of possible trouble. After a buy signal followed by a momentum divergence, tighten your stops to just beneath a recent low. After a sell signal followed by a momentum divergence, tighten your stops to just above a recent high. Follow the rules for entry stops (described later in this chapter) with this model. Use an initial 4 percent stop-loss system to protect against indicator failure.

OSCILLATOR-BASED SYSTEM

If you prefer an overbought/oversold system to time your trades, use Wilder's RSI:14 (daily). Follow the rules described earlier in the text. If the market is in an up trend as defined by point-and-figure charts, go long on buy signals and to cash on sell signals. If the market is in a down trend, go short on sell signals and cover your shorts and go to cash on buy signals. In an up trend, look for the market to get oversold. Buy as the RSI penetrates the 40 percent level to the upside. Then, wait for a bearish divergence taking two or more weeks to form, followed by a penetration of the 80 percent level before you sell out to cash. In a down trend, look for the market to get overbought. Sell short on a simple sell signal and a downside penetration of the 60 percent level. Then, wait for a bullish divergence taking at least two weeks to form, followed by an upside penetration of the 20 percent level to close out your shorts and go to cash. Use 4 percent exit stops, but ignore the entry-stop system (described later in this chapter).

To avoid being whipsawed, it probably is vital that you wait for divergences between the RSI and the index in question before you trade contrary to the major trend of the market. With this model, you may get stopped out of many trades. But your profits on successful trades should be substantial.

COMBINATION OF A TREND-FOLLOWING AND OSCILLATOR SYSTEM

This model combines both the DIOSC and the RSI in what, theoretically, should be a superior timing system. Here, you choose between the overbought/oversold and trend-following systems (previously described) based on Wilder's ADXR. (See Wilder's text, *New Concepts in Technical Trading Systems*, for computational details.) If the market is in an up trend as defined by point-and-figure charts, go long on buy signals and to cash on sell signals. If the market is in a down trend, go short on sell signals and cover your shorts and go to cash on buy signals.

If the ADXR is above 25, the market is in a trending mode and should be traded using trend-following indicators such as the DIOSC. If it is 20 or below, the market is oscillating and should be traded using overbought/oversold indicators such as RSI:14 (daily). In between, the ADXR does not give reliable signals. Use a 4 percent exit-stop system. Use the entry-stop system only when the ADXR is above 25.

CYCLE-BASED MODEL

If you are impressed by cycle theory, use fast Fourier transform to identify the three strongest cycles in the market and then enter these cycles' lengths into Larry Williams's Ultimate Oscillator. (This indicator frequently is found in sophisticated technical analysis software systems such as those containing the fast Fourier transform routine.) If the market is in an up trend as defined by point-and-figure charts, go long on buy signals and to cash on sell signals. If the market is in a down trend, go short on sell signals and cover your shorts and go to cash on buy signals.

Use lines of support and resistance on the oscillator. Look for both bullish and bearish divergences to warn you of an approaching turn in the market. Then, when the oscillator violates a line of resistance, you have a buy signal. When the oscillator violates a line of support, you have a sell signal. Use the entry-stop system and the 4 percent exit-stop system with this model.

SYSTEM COMBINING SENTIMENT AND MOMENTUM

If you are looking for a contrarian system to time the market, use *Investor's Intelligence* data along with William O'Neill's parameters (described in Chapter 5). If the market is in an up trend as defined by point-and-figure charts, go long on buy signals and to cash on sell signals. If the market is in a down trend, go short on sell signals and cover your shorts and go to cash on buy signals.

Wait for confirmation from RSI:14 (daily) before you trade. Markets can and do get overbought (or oversold) for long periods of time. Waiting for momentum failure before you trade will cut down on the number of false signals. Remember also to wait for divergences lasting two weeks or more before you trade contrary to the major trend. Again, use initial 4 percent exit stops to guard against model failure.

JAPANESE CANDLESTICKS, BOLLINGER BANDS AND STOCHASTICS

Plot daily candlesticks along with a 20-day simple moving average of daily closing prices and volatility bands at a distance of two standard deviations. If the market is in an up trend as defined by point-and-market is in a down trend, go short on sell signals and cover your shorts and go to cash on buy signals. Look for reversal signals when the market approaches either the 20-day SMA or the volatility bands. Use a five-day slow stochastic to confirm those signals.

ENTRY STOPS

To optimize your entry into the market, you should consider a system of entry stops that tells you exactly when to trade. If you receive buy signals from your indicators, you enter your buy order when the market penetrates above the high for the previous two days on an intraday basis *and* today's close is higher than yesterday's close and higher than today's opening. If you receive a series of sell signals, you enter your sell short order when the market penetrates below the low for the previous two days *and* today's close is lower than yesterday's close and lower than today's opening. This system is precise and needs careful explanation.

If you look at three days, day number one, day number two and day number three, you can get the intraday high, low, open and close for the first two days from your daily newspaper. Assume that you are getting buy signals from your indicators. If, during the third day, the market trends above the **print high** for both the first and the second days, you prepare to enter a buy order. If not, you drop the first day and add day number four and continue as before. (Day number two now becomes day number one, etc.)

You do not want to go long, however, if the market opens higher than it closes. This often is a classic **reversal day** and suggests a decline is likely. You also do not want to sell short if today's close is higher than the open (see Figure 11.1). Thus, you must wait for the market to close to decide what to do the following day. Those who can monitor the market during the last 15 minutes of trading (i.e., between 3:45 P.M. and 4:00 P.M. EST) might use the price at 3:45 P.M. as the unofficial closing price and enter the trade before the close of business at 4:00 P.M. Watch carefully, however, to see that the current trend of the market at closing time does not invalidate your signal.

In the absence of obvious stop-loss points from price charts or trend channels, 4 percent exit stops seem appropriate for mutual fund

FIGURE 11.1 Two-Day Entry Stops

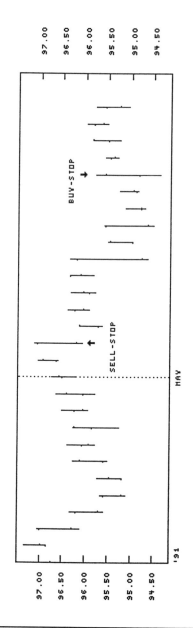

traders. That way, if, in the first four weeks of a trade, the market declines 4 percent or more below the point at which you bought into the mutual fund, you sell out to cash. After four weeks, use a four-week trailing stop to lock in some of the profits that already have been earned. (By definition, the four-week stop could not be lower than the entry stop. Otherwise, you would have been stopped-out of your long position.)

In any case, it is vital that you never initiate a trade without knowing exactly when you would exit the trade and take a small loss! You must identify stop-loss points before you initiate the trade. In those instances in which your signals are incorrect, you will limit your losses to a predetermined level.

NEED FOR CONFIRMATION

These models provide the reader with a series of alternatives to explore. In all six cases, pay close attention to a ten-day SMA of advancing minus declining stocks, a ten-day SMA of up minus down volume and a five-day SMA of new highs minus new lows for confirmation of signals based on your models. If you get a buy signal from a model but these indicators have not yet turned positive, be suspicious of that signal. If you get a sell signal from a model but these indicators have not yet turned negative, be suspicious of that sell signal. Also pay attention to the characteristics of major market tops and bottoms (described at the end of Chapter 10). These may help to warn you of times to tighten your stops or hedge your portfolio through the purchase of put or call options.

SUPPORT AND RESISTANCE

In addition to the rules included with each model, look for the market to violate a downwardly sloping line of resistance before acting on a buy signal or to violate an upwardly sloping line of support before acting on a sell signal. This additional rule should help you avoid being whipsawed by false signals.

STOCK-PICKING STRATEGIES

For those small investors who prefer individual stocks to mutual funds, the market holds out the prospect of even greater rewards. The strategies that can deliver excess profits, however, require increased effort. As with market timing, stock-picking strategies focus on either fundamental or technical analysis. The small investor should focus the bulk of his or her attention on small growth companies that often are overlooked by large, institutional investors.

Most stock-picking methods have several things in common, e.g., emphasis on small company growth stocks that have a strong five-year pattern of earnings growth, good relative strength, some institutional sponsorship, a hot product, relatively small capitalization, low debt-to-equity ratio and increasing market share.

VALUE LINE INVESTMENT SURVEY

For the past 26 years, the *Value Line Investment Survey* has been recommending stocks to its subscribers based on an analysis of both fundamental and technical characteristics. Typically, *Value Line* rates some 1,700 stocks according to two main criteria: timeliness and safety. One hundred stocks are rated in category one for timeliness, i.e., stocks that are most appropriate for immediate purchase. Three hundred stocks are rated number two. Nine hundred stocks are rated

TABLE 11.1 *Value Line* Performance

Group	26 Years	5 Years	1990
1	+15,641%	+63%	−10.4%
2	+ 1,334	+53	−10.2
3	+ 99	− 6	−24.4
4	− 65	−37	−33.7
5	− 98	−72	−45.5

SOURCE: As reported on the April 5, 1991, edition of "Wall Street Week" with Louis Rukeyser.

number three. Three hundred stocks are rated number four and 100 stocks are rated number five, i.e., the least timely stocks that might be purchased. Similar ratings are assigned for safety. Table 11.1 reviews the record of those rankings.

What accounts for this extraordinary record? Is it simply an anomaly, as some academicians have suggested? Or is it a sign that it is possible to beat the broader market averages? The 26-year record of the *Value Line Investment Survey* (as shown in Table 11.1) would seem to go well beyond anything attributable to random events. The fact that *Value Line* looks at earnings growth as well as relative strength in its analysis also suggests that these variables should be an important part of any stock-selection strategy.

WILLIAM O'NEILL

One of the best stock-selection systems is that developed by William O'Neill of *Investor's Business Daily*, modified slightly by David Ryan. Ryan has suggested concentrating your assets into a small number of stocks, e.g., five to eight, to be able to follow them closely. This runs the risk of lack of diversification but has been one of the keys to Ryan's outstanding performance in winning the U.S. Trading Championship.[4]

Ryan looks for stocks with strong relative strength and strong earnings growth, i.e., at least 80 percent.[5] He looks for strong stocks in strong industries. He wants stocks that have a relatively small number of shares and some institutional sponsorship. He also wants the volume in those stocks to be picking up on rallies and drying up on declines. Ryan basically buys on a breakout from a base of at least seven to eight weeks' duration using 7 percent stop-loss orders to protect his position. He does not like to buy stocks that are extended more than 10 percent from their bases. He expects to be right on 50 to 60 percent of his picks and seldom stays in a lagging stock very long. He likes to buy at the pivot point that generally is higher than other stock pickers might like. He explains that he is looking for evidence that the market has begun to recognize the value of this particular stock. He endorses William O'Neill's CANSLIM system, described in detail in O'Neill's book, *How To Make Money in Stocks*.

NEWSLETTERS

Those who lack the time to perform their own initial screening of the thousands of stocks that trade in the various markets might consider subscribing to two or three newsletters such as *John Bollinger's Capital Growth Newsletter*, the *Zweig Forecast*, Charles Allmon's *Growth Stock Outlook* or Al Frank's *Prudent Speculator*. You also might read the *Value Line Investment Survey* for ideas. Then, screen those picks for the characteristics described in William O'Neill's book. Trade blocks of 100 to 500 shares to reduce commission costs.

STOCK TIMING WITH
POINT-AND-FIGURE CHARTS

To simplify the problem of deciding when to buy or sell the stocks identified through the CANSLIM method or from your favorite market newsletter, consider using point-and-figure charts. Look to buy stocks when the broader market averages have penetrated above their bearish resistance lines (or still are above their bullish support lines). You should look for stocks that have generated a relative-strength buy signal. These are stocks that should outperform the broader market averages over the next year or so. Then, make sure that these stocks still are above their own bullish support line. This ensures that the specific stock also is in an up trend. Buy signals then are generated by breakouts above double or triple top formations. Sell out to cash on sell signals.

If the broader market has been in a down trend and is below its bearish resistance line, look for stocks that have generated a relative-strength sell signal to sell short. Make sure that the stock is below its bearish resistance line so that it, too, is in a down trend. Then, sell it short when it breaks below a double or triple bottom. Cover your shorts on buy signals.

Obviously, the point-and-figure system is much more complicated than has been suggested in this brief example. The beauty of the system, however, is in the clarity of its signals.

Endnotes

1. Bruce Babcock, Jr., *The Dow Jones-Irwin Guide to Trading Systems* (Homewood, Ill.: Dow Jones-Irwin, 1989).
2. Ibid., p. 69.
3. Ibid., p. 70.
4. Roman Zadeh runs a contest that he calls the "U.S. Trading and Investing Championships." Ryan has been the "most consistent winner" in the $50,000 stock division, according to an article by John Liscio in *Barron's*, 10 July 1989: 13. Ryan averaged 110 percent profits per year over the four previous years.
5. Based on comments on the "*Investor's Daily* Business Report," FNN, 28 August 1989.

12

A Simple Model That Works: FTS

My favorite market-timing model is based on futures traders' sentiment (FTS). It is the product of extensive back-testing and has been used in real-time trading since 1 January 1989. As with any model, it is far from perfect, but it does represent a substantial improvement on the buy-and-hold strategy. It also is competitive with some of the best intermediate-term market-timing systems that are available.

FUTURES TRADERS' SENTIMENT

Futures traders' sentiment is gathered by the Hadady Corporation and is available on a daily basis. You can use the weekly data published in *Barron's* on Mondays that is available by hotline on the previous Friday mornings. You want the information for stock index traders.

Calculate a 26-period simple moving average of the Friday data. Then, calculate trading bands at a distance of one standard deviation from the moving average. Round off calculations to the nearest tenth. When the weekly reading drops below the minus-one standard deviation band, you get a buy signal. When the weekly reading rises above the plus-one standard deviation band, you get a sell signal.

This system is most reliable when the market is in a broad trading range or is oscillating around a rising (or a falling) trendline. It works best when the ADXR is below 20 or when the weekly RSI:14 has been oscillating between the 40 and 60 percent bands for several weeks. Fortunately, these conditions exist quite frequently in the market.

This system does not work well during a strongly trending phase of the market such as the start of a new bull market, the start of a new bear market, during the blowoff phase of an old bull market or in the final capitulation phase of an older bear market. Unfortunately, these are precisely the times when a lot of money is made (or lost) in a very few months. That is why the use of mental stop-loss orders is extremely important.

WHY FUTURES TRADERS' SENTIMENT WORKS

Futures traders are among the most sophisticated market players. They trade contracts (futures) that have no systematic bias against the short side. There are no dividends paid or dividends owed. The time horizon of futures traders is typically a few days to a few weeks, i.e., not long enough for the market's long-term upward bias to affect prices by a significant amount. When any group of players becomes excessively optimistic or pessimistic, however, it usually is wrong.

Futures traders' sentiment is normally distributed, i.e., it is tightly clustered about its mean, symmetrical and strongly peaked and has very small tails on both sides of the mean. Thus, parametric statistical measures such as standard deviations are appropriate. The mean for this data is 50.4 (versus a median of 50), while the standard deviation is 7.7.

TIME DECAY OF TRADING SIGNALS

You should expect that 80 percent of all successful FTS trades will become profitable within the first two weeks after the signal was generated. If, however, the market refuses to behave as expected, the chances of signal failure increase with time. After two weeks, unprofitable signals turn out to be profitable only 50 percent of the time.

STOP-LOSS SYSTEM

Because any system can fail miserably at times, you must protect yourself against substantial losses. Use a 4 percent stop-loss system based on the point of entry for long and short trades. Thus, if at any time after you enter a long trade the market reverses 4 percent below your original entry point but futures traders' sentiment has not given a sell signal, exit the trade and go to cash. If at any time after you enter a short trade the market reverses 4 percent above your original entry point but futures traders' sentiment has not given a buy signal, exit the trade and go to cash.

In the hands of an experienced trader, more appropriate places to establish stops are possible. For example, FTS flashed a buy signal on 28 June 1991 as the DJIA closed at 2,906.75. For the past three and one-half months, the market had oscillated between 2,829.21 on the downside and 3,057.47 on the upside. An experienced trader would have expected a possible rise to 3,058 but would have set a mental stop at 2,829. Thus, if the DJIA closed below 2,829 for two consecutive days, that trader might have sold out of the position, avoiding further losses. That would establish the downside risk as approximately 2.67 percent, while the upside potential for the trade appeared to be 5.19 percent. Based on the fact that 79 percent of all FTS signals have turned out to be profitable, you might calculate the expected reward-risk ratio as the probable gain multiplied by the probability of the signal being profitable divided by the probable loss multiplied by the probability of the signal being unprofitable or $(5.19\% \times .79) \div (2.67\% \times .21) = 4.10 \div 0.56$ or approximately 7.3 to 1.

PERFORMANCE

How well did the basic model work? Looking just at the buy and sell signals (without considering the 4 percent stop-loss system), the model performed extraordinarily well.[1] Table 12.1 contains initial buy or sell signals (but ignores continuation signals) for 20 February 1987 through 1 November 1991.[2]

From 20 February 1987 through 1 November 1991, the capital appreciation earned by the FTS model was almost twice that earned by a buy-and-hold strategy. Over the past four-and-three-quarter years, there were 24 completed trades, i.e., one every ten weeks, on average. There were 19 successful trades and 5 unsuccessful trades. Thus,

79 percent of all trades were profitable. The best trade made 12.8 percent, while the worst trade lost 21.9 percent.

Figure 12.1, a weekly chart of the DJIA from 20 February 1987 through 1 November 1991, contains a record of all signals listed in Table 12.1. (Buy signals have been represented by arrows pointing upward, while sell signals have been represented by arrows pointing downward.)

Because most no-load mutual fund investors would not sell short on sell signals, the profitability of long trades is especially important. Over the past four-and-three-quarter years, there have been 12 long trades, 11 of which were profitable. Assuming you bought into a no-load fund that resembled the DJIA on buy signals and sold out to cash on sell signals, you would have gained 45 percent through use of the FTS model versus 35.3 percent for the buy-and-hold strategy.

While historical tests are suggestive, the real test of any system has to be in real time, i.e., after the model has been created. A real-time test of the model from 3 January 1989 to 1 November 1991 produced a capital appreciation of 56.6 percent for both long and short trades versus 42.5 percent for the buy-and-hold strategy. (In Figure 12.1, these signals are represented by the last 13 arrows.) Seventy-five percent of all signals were profitable, although some were only marginally so. All losses were 5.3 percent or less. The ratio of the best win to the worst loss was 1.6 to 1. The average gain on winning trades was 4.6 percent, while the average loss was 3 percent on unprofitable signals. All buy signals were profitable, while only three out of six sell signals were profitable. An investor who followed this system would have been in money market funds 105 weeks out of 247 or 43 percent of the time. The extra income earned in a money market fund as compared to the dividends earned by a buy-and-hold strategy would have been an added bonus.

SHARPE RATIO

Most investors hope to maximize their profits while minimizing their risks. One systematic measure of the relationship between risk and reward is the Sharpe ratio.[3] The Sharpe ratio can be used to

TABLE 12.1   Record of Initial Buy and Sell Signals*

| | | | SUMMARY OF SIGNALS | | | |
| | | | 26- | | Profit | |
Date	DJIA	FTS	Week	Signal	(Loss)	Compounded
02/20/87	2235.24	68	54.8	SELL	0.9306	0.9306
04/03/87	2390.34	45	57.7	BUY	1.1235	1.0455
08/14/87	2685.43	66	53.8	SELL	1.0462	1.0938
09/04/87	2561.38	34	52.5	BUY	0.7807	0.8539
12/24/87	1999.67	63	46.0	SELL	1.0046	0.8578
05/13/88	1990.55	39	49.2	BUY	1.0571	0.9068
06/17/88	2104.20	61	50.4	SELL	1.0205	0.9254
07/22/88	2060.99	43	50.8	BUY	1.0282	0.9515
08/05/88	2119.13	59	50.4	SELL	1.0480	0.9972
08/26/88	2017.43	39	50.1	BUY	1.0823	1.0793
10/21/88	2183.50	59	51.5	SELL	1.0533	1.1368
11/11/88	2067.03	38	51.6	BUY	1.1278	1.2822
02/03/89	2331.25	57	51.6	SELL	1.0161	1.3029
03/31/89	2293.62	38	45.4	BUY	1.0385	1.3530
05/05/89	2381.96	50	44.1	SELL	0.9371	1.2679

compare the performance of two different market-timing systems, portfolio managers or market indexes.

To compute the Sharpe ratio, you must know the average annual gains for a timing system, the standard deviation of those gains and the average interest rate of three-month Treasury bills over that same period. When you calculate this ratio, you are asking: Over a year's time, how did a timing model compare to a buy-and-hold strategy? While some analysts publish monthly risk-adjusted returns, many readers may find that less useful than calculations based on annualized data.

One danger in such calculations is that results may depend on particular starting and ending dates chosen by the analyst to illustrate the success of that system. To minimize this effect, you can mark the portfolio's value to the Friday closing price of the appropriate index

TABLE 12.1   Record of Initial Buy and Sell Signals* (continued)

			SUMMARY OF SIGNALS			
			26-		Profit	
Date	DJIA	FTS	Week	Signal	(Loss)	Compounded
06/23/89	2531.87	41	47.2	BUY	1.0617	1.3461
08/18/89	2687.97	62	47.9	SELL	0.9996	1.3455
10/20/89	2689.14	44	51.3	BUY	1.0313	1.3875
01/05/90	2773.25	57	51.5	SELL	1.0772	1.4946
01/26/90	2559.23	43	51.7	BUY	1.0617	1.5868
04/06/90	2717.12	57	49.8	SELL	1.0002	1.5871
08/10/90	2716.60	45	53.7	BUY	1.0420	1.6538
02/08/91	2830.69	53	47.0	SELL	0.9731	1.6094
06/28/91	2906.75	39	52.5	BUY	1.0515	1.6923
11/01/91	3056.35	52	44.0	SELL		

Timing Strategy   69.2
Buy-and-Hold Strategy   36.7
Ratio   1.9

*Note that adjustments were not made for slippage, i.e., the difference between the closing price on the day on which the signal was generated and the day on which the trade was made. For most no-load mutual fund investors trading $15,000 or less, most no-load mutual funds would process your trades without any difficulty. For very wealthy investors with much larger sums of money, however, you might be forced to trade over several days' time or to rely on more than one mutual fund family. The latter obviously is preferable.

(in this case the DJIA). Then, look to see how the portfolio grew over a series of overlapping, yearlong periods that can be constructed out of that data. Compute average, annual gains by dividing the price of the DJIA for week 53 by its price for week 1, week 54 by week 2, etc. This allows you to calculate average, annual gains from the timing system that eliminate the effect of specific starting and ending dates.

With 233 weeks of data from 20 February 1987 through 26 July 1991, 181 annualized periods can be constructed. Over those periods, the DJIA averaged a capital appreciation of 7 percent. (Figures have been rounded to the nearest tenth for the sake of the reader. Calculations, however, were based on rounding to the third decimal place.)

FIGURE 12.1   FTS Buy and Sell Signals, 1987–1991

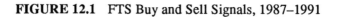

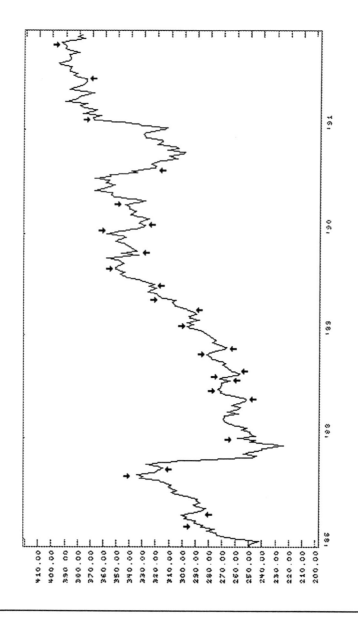

This was only 0.2 percent better than the three-month Treasury-bill rate of 6.8 percent. The standard deviation of these 181 periods was 14.5 percent. That gives a Sharpe ratio of 0.016. In short, the average buy-and-hold investor was very poorly compensated for the risk he or she took in the stock market from 20 February 1987 through 26 July 1991.

For the FTS model (including both long and short trades), the average annual gains were 16.4 percent with a standard deviation of 19.6 percent. Thus, while risks were higher, so were rewards. Was the extra reward worth the extra risk? Subtracting the 6.8 percent Treasury-bill rate from the average, annual capital appreciation of 16.4 percent and dividing by the standard deviation produces a Sharpe ratio of 0.492. This means that someone following the timing model earned substantially more money at significantly less risk than someone following a buy-and-hold strategy.

On the other hand, what would have happened if the worst possible period to evaluate the model's performance was chosen? For example, a disastrous buy signal issued on 4 September 1987 lost 22 percent as a result of the market crash. Furthermore, the buy signal generated on 10 August 1990 and the sell signal generated on 8 February 1991 were particularly weak. (That buy signal earned 2.6 percent, while that sell signal lost 2.7 percent.) Thus, we might evaluate the performance of the model from 4 September 1987 through 26 June 1991 as a potential worst-case scenario.

From 4 September 1987 through 28 June 1991, the FTS model had an average, annual capital appreciation of 21.3 percent for both long and short trades versus 11.1 percent for the buy-and-hold strategy. Total capital appreciation was 48.1 percent versus 13.5 percent for the market. Seventy-five percent of all signals were profitable. The standard deviation for the FTS model was 17.9 percent versus 12.4 percent for the buy-and-hold approach. With an average Treasury-bill rate of 7 percent, this gives a Sharpe ratio of 0.799 for the timing system and 0.331 for the buy-and-hold strategy. Thus, even when you base your calculations on what appear to be the worst series of signals from the model, it still outperformed the market by a substantial margin.

A RANDOM WALK?

What are the chances that the model's performance was attributable to luck? With 24 completed buy and sell signals from 20 February 1987 to 1 November 1991, you can test for statistical reliability using a chi-square test. The chi-square test is used by statisticians to measure nonparametric distributions. It is found in any standard statistics book.

To test any timing system, you must know how long the interval between one signal and another might have been. For example, with FTS, the average signal lasted ten weeks before you got a reverse signal. Over that period, the DJIA was up 67 percent of the time. Thus, you would expect that 67 percent of all random buy signals would have been profitable, while only 33 percent of random sell signals would have been profitable. In this case, 11 out of 12 of those buy signals were profitable. Was that a matter of luck? A chi-square of 3.3 with one degree of freedom indicates that the results are statistically significant at the 90 percent confidence level. Thus, the odds are nine to one that such results are not a matter of chance.

If sell signals were tested in the same way, you would expect that 67 percent of all sell signals would have been unprofitable and only 33 percent would have been profitable. In this case, 7 out of 12 sell signals were profitable. This gives a chi-square of 3.48 with one degree of freedom, which is statistically significant at the 90 percent confidence level. This means that the odds are nine to one that such results are not a matter of chance.

Obviously, some times the model worked better than others. What accounts for these differences? Although futures traders' sentiment is normally distributed over the long run, at times, the data is skewed. In such cases, theory suggests that the use of a standard deviation as the trigger point might not work very well. When the data was normally distributed and when the sample mean approximated the population mean, however, this model worked very well.

Twelve signals were generated at times when the sample mean fell within 2 percent of the theoretical population mean of 50 percent. In all 12 of these cases, the signals generated by FTS were profitable. Moreover, in such cases, the average gain per signal was 5 percent and the compounded profit from these signals was 79.2 percent. When the sample mean fell outside that range, there were seven successful signals and five unsuccessful signals. The average gain per signal was –0.1 percent and the compounded gain from all signals was –5.6 percent.

The chi-square for signals generated when the sample mean fell within 2 percent of the theoretical population mean was 3.33, which is statistically significant at the 90 percent confidence level. Thus, the odds are nine to one that this rule will improve the performance of the FTS model. For the average investor, this means that the closer the 26-week SMA of futures traders' sentiment is to the theoretical population mean of 50 percent, the more likely that signal is to be profitable. It also means that when the 26-week moving average of futures traders' sentiment falls outside that range, the model's signals should not be trusted without confirmation from other indicators.

Two possible modifications of this system might be worth considering. The first would be to trade only when the FTS model gave buy or sell signals and the 26-week SMA of futures traders' sentiment fell within the 48.0 to 52.0 range. In such cases, over the period 20 February 1987 through 1 November 1991, the model produced a theoretical capital appreciation of 64.2 percent versus 35.3 percent for the buy-and-hold strategy.

A second modification might be to buy into the market on any buy signal and sell only on a sell signal if the 26-week SMA of futures traders' sentiment fell within the 48.0 to 52.0 range. This rule would have produced a theoretical capital appreciation of 87.8 percent versus 35.3 percent for the buy-and-hold strategy over the past four and one-half years. There were 11 such trades, 10 of which were profitable. The best win was 11.4 percent and the worst loss was 5.9 percent. The low number of trades per year should allow this system to be used even with mutual fund families that restrict investors to no more than one trade per quarter. This rule would seem appropriate only when the market was above a long-term line of support extending back several years.

The low level of time and effort required to maintain this system (about ten minutes per week) justifies it for most no-load mutual fund investors. The addition of a 4 percent stop-loss system should improve the model's performance.

There is, of course, no guarantee that futures traders' sentiment will continue to work as well in the future. The success of a variety of other sentiment indicators, however, suggests that the prospects for market timing based on investor sentiment are excellent. Remember, past results are no guarantee of future performance.

Endnotes

1. Appendix III contains a complete listing of the weekly *Bullish Consensus* reading for stocks, the date that data was available by hotline, the 26-week simple moving average, the standard deviation, the plus-one criterion (i.e., the sell level) and the minus-one criterion (i.e., the buy signal).
2. Starting dates were based on the availability of machine-readable data for both the *Bullish Consensus* and the DJIA.
3. A discussion of the Sharpe ratio and its limitations can be found in an article by Jack Schwager, "Alternatives to Sharpe Ratio: Better Measure of Performance," *Futures* (March 1985): 56–58.

Conclusion

Investing in no-load mutual funds will not make you rich overnight. But a lifelong habit of regular investment through dollar cost averaging can pave the way for a safe and secure retirement or it can greatly ease the burden of paying for a child's education. Diversification of your assets is an excellent way to reduce the volatility of your portfolio. But you must base asset-allocation decisions on your time to retirement as well as your risk tolerance.

For most passive investors, dollar cost averaging combined with an asset-allocation strategy makes great sense. Active investors who have a self-directed Individual Retirement Account (IRA) might consider following Gary Zin's suggestion that you buy shares in no-load mutual funds rated in the top 20 percent for recent performance. Those with a self-directed, tax-deferred 401(k) or 403(b), SRA (Supplemental Retirement Annuity), TSA (Tax-Sheltered Annuity) or other qualified retirement annuity account might consider allocating their assets between blue chips and secondary stocks as suggested in Chapter 2. For the active investor seeking professional advice, a number of investment newsletters can ease the problem of choosing individual stocks or mutual funds. Contact the publisher of a newsletter and ask for sample copies. Check a recent issue of the *Hulbert Financial Digest* for performance rankings.

For the aggressive investor who wants to make his or her own decisions, additional opportunities for capital appreciation are available through stock-market timing. After you have diversified your portfolio based on your risk tolerance and age to retirement, you may want to experiment with market timing with some of your risk capital.

Each of us has a different learning style, a different time horizon and a different risk tolerance. No one approach is right for everyone. Regardless of how you decide to invest, follow that system for several months on paper until you are confident that it is both safe and reliable and meets your personal needs. Also, be sure never to trade more than you can afford to lose. Because even the best market-timing model will fail on occasion, you must protect your assets through the disciplined use of stop-loss orders.

This book began as a series of personal notes intended to help me think my way through the morass of advice on the stock market. It ended with the discovery of a variety of very interesting and potentially useful market-timing techniques. Despite the claims of the skeptics, stock-market timing works. The efficient market hypothesis is a half-truth: It consoles the lazy and creates opportunities for the hardworking to find opportunities in the market where the efficient market hypothesis does not apply. A combination of good stock-picking, market timing and disciplined trading techniques should beat the daylights out of a buy-and-hold strategy. But that path is difficult and requires discipline, courage and hard work. At the very least, this book should provide you with a knowledge of the technical tools used by market analysts to judge the general health and condition of the stock market. It may even start you off in the direction of developing your own highly profitable market-timing systems.

Appendix I:
Profitability Tests

PROFITABILITY TESTS
03/17/89 to 03/08/91

TEST 1: *Directional Movement*
(Both Long and Short Positions)
DJIA
Directional Oscillator

Total long trades: 11	Total short trades: 12
Profitable longs: 6 (55%)	Profitable shorts: 2 (17%)
Total short stops: 0	Total long stops: 0
Biggest gain: 364.4	Biggest loss: -144.4
Successive gains: 2	Successive losses: 3
Total gain/loss: 44.6	Average gain/loss: 1.9
Total gain/loss ($): -12.1	Total gain/loss (%): -1.2

TEST 2: M. A. Price Penetration
(Both Long and Short Positions)
DJIA
(20-Unit Moving Average of Security)

Total long trades: 22

Total short trades: 22

Profitable longs: 8 (36%)

Profitable shorts: 4 (18%)

Total short stops: 0

Total long stops: 0

Biggest gain: 295.1

Biggest loss: -144.4

Successive gains: 2

Successive losses: 10

Total gain/loss: -192.5

Average gain/loss: -4.4

Total gain/loss ($): -92.00

Total gain/loss (%): -9.2

TEST 3: M. A. Indicator Penetration
(Both Long and Short Positions)
DJIA
MACD
(9-Unit Moving Average of Indicator)

Total long trades: 18

Total short trades: 17

Profitable longs: 7 (39%)

Profitable shorts: 3 (18%)

Total short stops: 0

Total long stops: 0

Biggest gain: 311.4

Biggest loss: -185.3

Successive gains: 1

Successive losses: 7

Total gain/loss: -69.5

Average gain/loss: -2.0

Total gain/loss ($): -61.4

Total gain/loss (%): -6.1

TEST 4: *Stochastic 20/80*
(Both Long and Short Positions)
DJIA
5%K 3%D Stochastic

Total long trades: 14	Total short trades: 27
Profitable longs: 9 (64%)	Profitable shorts: 10 (37%)
Total short stops: 17	Total long stops: 3
Biggest gain: 222.8	Biggest loss: -198.7
Successive gains: 2	Successive losses: 2
Total gain/loss: -195.60	Average gain/loss: -4.8
Total gain/loss ($): -96.10	Total gain/loss (%): -9.6

TEST 5: *Price Rate-of-Change*
(Both Long and Short Positions)
DJIA
12 Price Rate-of-Change

Total long trades: 9	Total short trades: 3
Profitable longs: 2 (22.2%)	Profitable shorts: 1 (33%)
Total short stops: 1	Total long stops: 7
Biggest gain: 276.7	Biggest loss: -184.1
Successive gains: 2	Successive losses: 2
Total gain/loss: 154.15	Average gain/loss: 12.8
Total gain/loss ($): 51.66	Total gain/loss (%): 5.2

TEST 6: *Parabolic SAR*
(Both Long and Short Positions)
DJIA
0.02/0.20 Parabolic

Total long trades: 24	Total short trades: 25
Profitable longs: 11 (46%)	Profitable shorts: 6 (24%)
Total short stops: 0	Total long stops: 0
Biggest gain: 272.3	Biggest loss: -125.6
Successive gains: 4	Successive losses: 6
Total gain/loss: -83.8	Average gain/loss: -1.7
Total gain/loss ($): -61.31	Total gain/loss (%): -6.1

Appendix II:
Futures Contracts

The would-be technical analyst must understand how futures contracts are traded and how index arbitrage affects the stock market. These contracts are so highly leveraged that they offer the prospects for enormous gains (and equally enormous losses). Avoid all futures, options on futures, options and commodity markets. These are for the well-heeled speculator, not for the average investor.

Futures contracts on commodities provide an opportunity for consumers of these commodities to lock in prices for some future date. For example, General Mills may want to ensure that it has 50,000 bushels of corn for its cereals at some specified price in six months' time. Purchasing corn futures contracts on the Chicago Board of Trade becomes the appropriate means of guaranteeing delivery at a specific time and price. Similarly, Ford Motor Corporation may want to be sure that it can ship automobiles from Detroit to Canada in six months for a specified price in U.S. dollars. Hedging currency transactions in the futures market becomes the appropriate means to ensure the company against currency volatility.

While demand for specific commodities may fluctuate seasonally, that demand still is relatively stable from week to week. But futures contracts also are traded by speculators. Perceived opportunities to make a speculative profit can rapidly drive the price of a futures contract up or down and can cause open interest to fluctuate substantially as speculators enter or exit the market.

Just as commodity traders can use futures contracts to hedge their risks or to speculate on price movements, stock-market investors can hedge their investment portfolios or can speculate on future price movements with stock index futures contracts.[1] If an institution fears a market decline, it can sell a futures contract against all or part of its portfolio. Then, if the market declines, it has reduced its exposure to the stock market and avoids all or part of the loss incurred to the buy-and-hold investor without incurring high transaction costs. But the hedger's entry into the futures market is balanced by the speculator's purchase of that contract.

INDEX ARBITRAGE

The equilibrium price of a futures contract is, theoretically, the cost of the underlying cash index plus the interest charge on borrowing that sum until the expiration date. The cost of carry is the cost of borrowing funds for the time to expiration of the contract less the accumulated dividends in that period. The formula for that relationship is:

$$365 \div m \times (F - S) \div S = r - d$$

where F is the index futures price, S is the cash index price, $(F - S)$ divided by S is called the basis, r is the annualized rate of interest, d is the annualized dividend yield and m is the number of days to maturity.[2] (Alternatively, John Bollinger suggests the formula: ((Treasury-bill rate minus yield) ÷ 365) × days to expiration.)[3]

Hans R. Stoll and Robert E. Whaley explain: "If the basis exceeds the net cost of carrying the index by more than the transaction costs, the arbitrager buys the index by buying some or all of the stocks in the index and sells futures. This is called long arbitrage."[4] Similarly, they explain: "If the basis is less than the net cost of carrying the index by enough to outweigh transaction costs, the arbitrager sells short the stocks in the index and buys index futures—a short arbitrage."[5]

Scalpers try to enter the market just before the futures premium hits the point at which long index arbitrage might be triggered and then exit the market after a brief but sharp rise. Similarly, scalpers will enter the market and sell a contract just before the futures premium hits the point at which short arbitrage might be triggered and then exit the market after a brief but sharp decline in prices.

Endnotes

1. Hans R. Stoll and Robert E. Whaley, *Expiration Day Effects of Index Options and Futures,* Monograph Series in Finance and Economics, Monograph 1986-3, Salomon Brothers Center for the Study of Financial Institutions, Graduate School of Business Administration, New York University, p. 14.
2. Ibid., p. 22.
3. "Count Down," FNN, 23 June 1989.
4. Stoll and Whaley, p. 22.
5. Ibid., p. 23.

Appendix III:
Bullish Consensus
Readings

Table III.1 contains a record of the *Bullish Consensus* readings for stock index traders since 2 January 1987. Note that this is Friday data, published the following Monday in *Barron's*. It also is available by 900 number on Friday mornings from the Hadady Corporation.

TABLE III.1 *Bullish Consensus*, 1987–1991 (Friday Data Only)

DATE	CLOSE	Weekly Data*	26-Week SMA	Standard Deviation	Plus 1	Minus 1	Signal
08/22/86	1887.80	65					
08/29/86	1898.34	66					
09/05/86	1899.75	58					
09/12/86	1758.72	58					
09/19/86	1762.65	34					
09/26/86	1769.69	33					
10/03/86	1774.18	32					
10/10/86	1793.17	36					
10/17/86	1837.04	46					
10/24/86	1832.26	40					

*Weekly data reprinted from Market Vane Corporation, P. O. Box 90490, Pasadena, CA 91109-0490, 818-441-8466. This material is copyrighted.

DATE	CLOSE	Weekly Data*	26-Week SMA	Standard Deviation	Plus 1	Minus 1	Signal
10/31/86	1877.81	48					
11/07/86	1886.53	59					
11/14/86	1873.59	70					
11/21/86	1893.56	51					
11/28/86	1914.23	64					
12/05/86	1924.78	66					
12/12/86	1912.26	56					
12/19/86	1928.85	57					
12/26/86	1930.40	60					
01/02/87	1927.31						
01/09/87	2005.91						
01/16/87	2076.63	63					
01/23/87	2101.52	64					
01/30/87	2158.04	65					
02/06/87	2186.87	63					
02/13/87	2183.35	58	54.7	11.8	66.5	42.8	
02/20/87	2235.24	68	54.8	11.9	66.7	42.8	Sell
02/27/87	2223.99	64	54.7	11.9	66.6	42.8	
03/06/87	2280.23	60	54.8	11.9	66.7	42.9	
03/13/87	2258.66	60	54.9	11.9	66.8	42.9	
03/20/87	2333.52	58	55.9	11.1	67.0	44.8	
03/27/87	2335.80	63	57.1	10.0	67.2	47.1	
04/03/87	2390.34	45	57.7	8.9	66.6	48.8	Buy
04/10/87	2338.78	56	58.5	7.6	66.1	50.9	
04/16/87	2275.99	37	58.1	8.5	66.6	49.7	Buy
04/24/87	2235.37	40	58.1	8.5	66.6	49.7	Buy
05/01/87	2280.40	42	57.9	8.8	66.7	49.0	Buy
05/08/87	2232.30	51	57.5	9.0	66.5	48.6	
05/15/87	2272.52	52	56.8	8.6	65.4	48.2	

DATE	CLOSE	Weekly Data*	26-Week SMA	Standard Deviation	Plus 1	Minus 1	Signal
05/22/87	2243.20	43	56.5	9.0	65.5	47.5	Buy
05/29/87	2291.57	48	55.8	9.0	64.8	46.8	
06/05/87	2326.15	51	55.2	8.8	63.9	46.4	
06/12/87	2377.73	63	55.5	8.9	64.4	46.5	
06/19/87	2420.85	59	55.5	8.9	64.5	46.6	
06/26/87	2436.86	64	55.7	9.1	64.8	46.6	
07/02/87	2436.70	55	55.7	8.9	64.6	46.8	
07/10/87	2455.99	56	55.7	8.7	64.4	47.0	
07/17/87	2510.04	59	55.5	8.6	64.1	46.9	
07/24/87	2485.33	48	54.9	8.5	63.5	46.4	
07/31/87	2572.07	45	54.2	8.5	62.7	45.7	Buy
08/07/87	2592.00	45	53.5	8.5	61.9	45.0	Buy
08/14/87	2685.43	66	53.8	8.8	62.6	45.0	Sell
08/21/87	2709.50	56	53.3	8.3	61.6	45.0	
08/28/87	2639.35	69	53.5	8.6	62.1	44.9	Sell
09/04/87	2561.38	34	52.5	9.3	61.8	43.2	Buy
09/11/87	2608.74	35	51.5	9.8	61.3	41.7	Buy
09/18/87	2524.64	36	50.7	10.2	60.9	40.5	Buy
09/25/87	2570.17	33	49.5	10.4	59.9	39.1	Buy
10/02/87	2640.99	42	49.4	10.5	59.9	38.9	
10/09/87	2482.21	38	48.7	10.6	59.3	38.1	Buy
10/16/87	2246.74	38	48.8	10.6	59.3	38.2	Buy
10/23/87	1950.76	27	48.3	11.3	59.6	37.0	Buy
10/30/87	1993.53	43	48.3	11.3	59.6	37.0	
11/06/87	1959.05	45	48.1	11.3	59.4	36.8	
11/13/87	1935.01	45	47.8	11.3	59.1	36.5	
11/20/87	1913.63	43	47.8	11.3	59.1	36.5	
11/27/87	1910.48	46	47.7	11.3	59.0	36.5	
12/04/87	1766.74	36	47.2	11.5	58.6	35.7	

DATE	CLOSE	Weekly Data*	26-Week SMA	Standard Deviation	Plus 1	Minus 1	Signal
12/11/87	1867.04	41	46.3	11.1	57.4	35.2	
12/18/87	1975.30	51	46.0	10.8	56.8	35.2	
12/24/87	1999.67	63	46.0	10.7	56.7	35.2	Sell
12/31/87	1938.83	58	46.1	10.9	56.9	35.2	Sell
01/08/88	1911.31		45.7	10.9	56.6	34.8	
01/15/88	1956.07	46	45.2	10.5	55.7	34.6	
01/22/88	1903.51	50	45.2	10.6	55.8	34.7	
01/29/88	1958.22	60	45.8	11.0	56.8	34.9	Sell
02/05/88	1910.48	57	46.3	11.2	57.5	35.1	
02/12/88	1983.26	46	45.5	10.4	55.9	35.1	
02/19/88	2014.59	52	45.4	10.3	55.6	35.1	
02/26/88	2023.21	58	44.9	9.4	54.3	35.5	Sell
03/04/88	2057.86	65	46.2	9.9	56.1	36.2	Sell
03/11/88	2034.98	59	47.1	10.0	57.1	37.1	Sell
03/18/88	2087.37	50	47.7	9.7	57.4	38.0	
03/25/88	1978.95	50	48.4	9.2	57.6	39.1	
03/31/88	1988.06	41	48.3	9.3	57.6	39.1	
04/08/88	2090.19	40	48.4	9.2	57.6	39.2	
04/15/88	2013.93	49	48.8	8.9	57.8	39.9	
04/22/88	2015.90	45	49.6	7.7	57.3	41.8	
04/29/88	2032.22	47	49.7	7.6	57.3	42.1	
05/06/88	2007.46	47	49.8	7.6	57.4	42.2	
05/13/88	1990.55	39	49.6	7.8	57.4	41.7	Buy
05/20/88	1952.59	51	49.9	7.7	57.6	42.2	
05/27/88	1956.44	43	49.8	7.8	57.6	42.0	
06/03/88	2071.30	52	50.4	7.3	57.7	43.1	
06/10/88	2101.71	43	50.5	7.2	57.6	43.3	Buy
06/17/88	2104.20	61	50.9	7.5	58.3	43.4	Sell
06/24/88	2142.96	59	50.7	7.2	58.0	43.5	Sell

DATE	CLOSE	Weekly Data*	26-Week SMA	Standard Deviation	Plus 1	Minus 1	Signal
07/01/88	2131.58	58	50.7	7.2	58.0	43.5	Sell
07/08/88	2106.15	58	51.0	7.2	58.2	43.8	
07/15/88	2129.45	62	51.6	7.5	59.1	44.1	Sell
07/22/88	2060.99	43	51.3	7.7	59.0	43.7	Buy
07/29/88	2128.73	46	50.8	7.5	58.3	43.3	
08/05/88	2119.13	59	50.9	7.6	58.5	43.3	Sell
08/12/88	2037.52	54	51.2	7.5	58.7	43.7	
08/19/88	2016.00	50	51.1	7.5	58.7	43.6	
08/26/88	2017.43	39	50.4	7.8	58.2	42.6	
09/02/88	2054.59	49	49.8	7.2	56.9	42.6	
09/09/88	2068.81	56	49.7	7.0	56.7	42.6	
09/16/88	2098.15	51	49.7	7.0	56.7	42.6	
09/23/88	2090.68	51	49.7	7.1	56.8	42.7	
09/30/88	2112.91	57	50.3	7.0	57.3	43.4	
10/07/88	2150.25	50	50.7	6.6	57.4	44.1	
10/14/88	2133.18	55	51.0	6.7	57.6	44.3	
10/21/88	2183.50	59	51.5	6.7	58.2	44.8	Sell
10/28/88	2149.89	51	51.7	6.7	58.3	45.0	
11/04/88	2142.00	47	51.7	6.7	58.3	45.0	
11/11/88	2067.03	38	51.6	6.8	58.4	44.9	Buy
11/18/88	2052.45	38	51.1	7.3	58.4	43.9	Buy
11/25/88	2074.68	33	50.7	7.9	58.7	42.8	Buy
12/02/88	2092.28	38	50.2	8.3	58.5	41.9	Buy
12/09/88	2143.49	40	50.1	8.4	58.5	41.6	Buy
12/16/88	2150.71	45	49.5	8.2	57.7	41.3	
12/23/88	2168.93	49	49.1	8.0	57.0	41.1	
12/30/88	2168.57		48.7	7.9	56.6	40.8	
01/06/89	2194.29	39	48.0	7.9	55.9	40.1	Buy
01/13/89	2226.07	44	47.2	7.4	54.6	39.9	

DATE	CLOSE	Weekly Data*	26-Week SMA	Standard Deviation	Plus 1	Minus 1	Signal
01/20/89	2235.36	43	47.2	7.4	54.6	39.9	
01/27/89	2322.86	49	47.4	7.4	54.7	40.0	
02/03/89	2331.25	57	47.3	7.2	54.5	40.0	Sell
02/10/89	2286.07	51	47.2	7.2	54.3	40.0	
02/17/89	2324.82	44	46.9	7.2	54.1	39.8	
02/24/89	2245.54	49	47.3	7.0	54.3	40.4	
03/03/89	2274.29	43	47.1	7.0	54.1	40.1	
03/10/89	2282.14	43	46.6	6.8	53.4	39.8	
03/17/89	2292.14	47	46.4	6.7	53.1	39.7	
03/23/89	2243.04	46	46.2	6.7	52.9	39.5	
03/31/89	2293.62	38	45.4	6.5	51.9	39.0	Buy
04/07/89	2304.80	47	45.3	6.4	51.7	38.9	
04/14/89	2337.06	41	44.8	6.1	50.9	38.6	
04/21/89	2409.46	42	44.1	5.4	49.5	38.7	
04/28/89	2418.80	48	44.0	5.3	49.2	38.7	
05/05/89	2381.96	50	44.1	5.4	49.4	38.7	Sell
05/12/89	2439.70	51	44.6	5.4	50.0	39.2	Sell
05/19/89	2501.10	58	45.4	5.8	51.2	39.6	Sell
05/26/89	2493.77	54	46.2	5.5	51.7	40.8	Sell
06/02/89	2490.63	54	46.9	5.4	52.3	41.5	Sell
06/09/89	2513.42	54	47.4	5.4	52.8	42.1	Sell
06/16/89	2486.38	47	47.5	5.4	52.9	42.2	
06/23/89	2531.87	41	47.2	5.5	52.7	41.7	Buy
06/30/89	2440.06	44	47.1	5.4	52.5	41.7	
07/07/89	2487.86	36	47.0	5.6	52.6	41.3	Buy
07/14/89	2554.82	49	47.2	5.6	52.8	41.5	
07/21/89	2607.36	50	47.4	5.6	53.0	41.9	
07/28/89	2635.24	50	47.5	5.6	53.0	41.9	
08/04/89	2653.45	50	47.2	5.3	52.5	41.9	

DATE	CLOSE	Weekly Data*	26-Week SMA	Standard Deviation	Plus 1	Minus 1	Signal
08/11/89	2683.99	51	47.2	5.3	52.5	41.9	
08/18/89	2687.97	62	47.9	6.0	53.9	41.9	Sell
08/25/89	2732.36	58	48.2	6.3	54.5	41.9	Sell
09/01/89	2752.09	60	48.9	6.6	55.5	42.3	Sell
09/08/89	2709.54	59	49.5	6.8	56.3	42.7	Sell
09/15/89	2674.58	55	49.8	6.8	56.6	43.0	
09/22/89	2681.61	54	50.1	6.8	57.0	43.3	
09/29/89	2692.82	47	50.5	6.4	56.9	44.0	
10/06/89	2785.52	51	50.6	6.4	57.0	44.2	
10/13/89	2569.26	56	51.2	6.1	57.3	45.0	
10/20/89	2689.14	44	51.3	6.0	57.3	45.2	Buy
10/27/89	2596.72	44	51.1	6.2	57.3	44.9	Buy
11/03/89	2629.51	48	51.0	6.2	57.2	44.8	
11/10/89	2625.61	45	50.8	6.3	57.1	44.5	
11/17/89	2652.66	48	50.4	6.2	56.6	44.3	
11/24/89	2675.55	48	50.2	6.1	56.3	44.1	
12/01/89	2747.65	45	49.8	6.2	56.0	43.7	
12/08/89	2731.23	50	49.7	6.1	55.8	43.6	
12/15/89	2739.55	52	49.9	6.1	56.0	43.8	
12/22/89	2711.39	51	50.3	5.8	56.1	44.4	
12/29/89	2727.00	56	50.7	5.8	56.5	45.0	
01/05/90	2773.25	57	51.5	5.1	56.6	46.5	Sell
01/12/90	2689.21	59	51.9	5.2	57.2	46.7	Sell
01/19/90	2677.90	50	51.9	5.2	57.2	46.7	
01/26/90	2559.23	43	51.7	5.5	57.2	46.1	Buy
02/02/90	2602.70	42	51.3	5.8	57.2	45.5	Buy
02/09/90	2648.20	47	51.2	5.9	57.1	45.3	
02/16/90	2635.59	42	50.4	5.7	56.1	44.7	Buy
02/23/90	2564.19	46	50.0	5.6	55.5	44.4	

DATE	CLOSE	Weekly Data*	26-Week SMA	Standard Deviation	Plus 1	Minus 1	Signal
03/02/90	2660.36	51	49.6	5.2	54.8	44.4	
03/09/90	2683.33	54	49.4	4.9	54.3	44.5	
03/16/90	2741.22	52	49.3	4.8	54.1	44.5	
03/23/90	2704.28	54	49.3	4.8	54.1	44.5	
03/30/90	2707.21	53	49.5	4.8	54.4	44.7	
04/06/90	2717.12	57	49.8	5.0	54.8	44.7	Sell
04/12/90	2751.88	59	49.9	5.2	55.1	44.7	Sell
04/20/90	2695.95	56	50.3	5.2	55.6	45.1	Sell
04/27/90	2645.05	53	50.7	5.1	55.8	45.6	
05/04/90	2710.36	51	50.8	5.0	55.9	45.8	
05/11/90	2801.58	51	51.0	4.9	55.9	46.1	
05/18/90	2818.75	58	51.4	5.0	56.5	46.4	Sell
05/25/90	2856.26	59	51.8	5.2	57.1	46.6	Sell
06/01/90	2900.97	62	52.5	5.4	57.9	47.1	Sell
06/08/90	2935.19	58	52.8	5.5	58.3	47.4	
06/15/90	2935.89	57	53.0	5.5	58.5	47.5	
06/22/90	2901.73	54	53.1	5.5	58.6	47.6	
06/29/90	2880.45	50	52.9	5.5	58.4	47.4	
07/06/90	2911.63	50	52.6	5.5	58.1	47.2	
07/13/90	2980.20	55	52.5	5.3	57.8	47.1	
07/20/90	2999.75	59	52.8	5.5	58.3	47.4	Sell
07/27/90	2930.94	55	53.3	5.1	58.4	48.2	
08/03/90	2917.33	54	53.7	4.5	58.3	49.2	
08/10/90	2758.91	45	53.7	4.7	58.3	49.0	Buy
08/17/90	2748.27	48	53.9	4.2	58.1	49.7	Buy
08/24/90	2656.44	44	53.8	4.4	58.2	49.4	Buy
08/31/90	2632.43	49	53.7	4.4	58.2	49.3	Buy
09/07/90	2628.22	51	53.6	4.5	58.1	49.2	
09/14/90	2625.74	53	53.7	4.5	58.1	49.2	

DATE	CLOSE	Weekly Data*	26-Week SMA	Standard Deviation	Plus 1	Minus 1	Signal
09/21/90	2576.29	51	53.5	4.5	58.0	49.1	
09/28/90	2485.64	48	53.3	4.6	58.0	48.7	Buy
10/05/90	2516.83	51	53.1	4.6	57.7	48.5	
10/12/90	2523.76	51	52.8	4.4	57.2	48.4	
10/19/90	2416.34	43	52.3	4.8	57.1	47.5	Buy
10/26/90	2436.14	45	52.0	5.0	57.0	47.0	Buy
11/02/90	2490.84	48	51.9	5.0	56.9	46.8	
11/09/90	2448.61	50	51.8	5.0	56.9	46.8	
11/16/90	2550.25	45	51.3	5.1	56.4	46.3	Buy
11/23/90	2527.23	48	50.9	4.8	55.8	46.1	
11/30/90	2559.65	47	50.3	4.3	54.7	46.0	
12/07/90	2590.10	45	49.8	4.2	54.0	45.7	Buy
12/14/90	2593.81	49	49.5	3.9	53.4	45.6	
12/21/90	2633.66	40	49.0	4.2	53.2	44.8	Buy
12/28/90	2629.21		49.0	4.3	53.3	44.7	
01/04/91	2566.09	44	48.7	4.4	53.1	44.3	Buy
01/11/91	2501.49	41	48.2	4.5	52.6	43.7	Buy
01/18/91	2646.78	39	47.4	4.2	51.6	43.1	Buy
01/25/91	2659.41	46	47.0	3.9	50.9	43.1	
02/01/91	2730.69	47	46.7	3.6	50.4	43.1	
02/08/91	2830.69	53	47.0	3.8	50.9	43.2	Sell
02/15/91	2934.65	61	47.6	4.7	52.3	42.8	Sell
02/22/91	2889.36	60	48.2	5.3	53.5	42.9	Sell
03/01/91	2909.90	58	48.6	5.6	54.2	42.9	Sell
03/08/91	2955.20	60	48.9	6.1	55.0	42.8	Sell
03/15/91	2948.27	59	49.2	6.4	55.5	42.8	Sell
03/22/91	2858.95	56	49.4	6.5	55.9	42.9	Sell
03/29/91	2917.57	59	49.8	6.8	56.6	43.0	Sell
04/05/91	2896.78	59	50.1	7.0	57.1	43.1	Sell

DATE	CLOSE	Weekly Data*	26-Week SMA	Standard Deviation	Plus 1	Minus 1	Signal
04/12/91	2920.79	57	50.4	7.1	57.5	43.2	
04/19/91	2965.59	57	50.9	7.1	58.0	43.8	
04/26/91	2912.38	60	51.5	7.2	58.7	44.3	Sell
05/03/91	2938.86	54	51.8	7.2	58.9	44.6	
05/10/91	2920.17	52	51.8	7.2	59.0	44.7	
05/17/91	2886.63	50	52.0	7.0	59.1	45.0	
05/24/91	2913.91	51	52.2	7.0	59.2	45.2	
05/31/91	3027.50	52	52.4	6.9	59.3	45.5	
06/07/91	2976.74	52	52.6	6.7	59.4	45.9	
06/14/91	3000.45	51	52.7	6.7	59.4	46.0	
06/21/91	2965.56	48	53.0	6.2	59.3	46.8	
06/28/91	2906.75	39	52.5	6.7	59.2	45.8	Buy
07/05/91	2932.47	41	52.4	6.9	59.3	45.5	Buy
07/12/91	2980.77	41	52.4	6.9	59.3	45.5	Buy
07/19/91	3016.32	46	52.7	6.5	59.1	46.2	Buy
07/26/91	2972.50	47	52.7	6.4	59.1	46.3	
08/02/91	3006.26	45	52.7	6.5	59.2	46.2	Buy
08/09/91	2996.20	42	52.3	6.8	59.1	45.5	Buy
08/16/91	2968.02	46	51.7	6.7	58.4	45.0	
08/23/91	3040.25	39	50.9	6.9	57.9	44.0	Buy
08/30/91	3017.67	39	50.2	7.2	57.3	43.0	Buy
09/06/91	3011.63	40	49.4	7.1	56.6	42.3	Buy
09/13/91	2985.69	39	48.7	7.1	55.8	41.5	Buy
09/20/91	3019.23	36	47.9	7.4	55.3	40.5	Buy
09/27/91	3006.04	38	47.1	7.3	54.3	39.8	Buy
10/04/91	2961.76	40	46.3	7.0	53.3	39.4	
10/11/91	2983.68	32	45.4	7.2	52.6	38.2	Buy
10/18/91	3077.15	38	44.7	6.9	51.6	37.8	
10/25/91	3004.92	44	44.0	6.1	50.2	37.9	
11/01/91	3056.35	52	44.0	6.0	50.0	37.9	Sell

Glossary

announcement effect A change in the discount rate that often convinces investors that the Federal Reserve System has changed its interest rate policy. This often leads to a significant market reaction over the next few days and weeks.

bear market A declining market. To be bearish about the market means to expect a sell-off ahead.

book value A calculation of a company's net worth based on assets minus liabilities.

bull market A rising market. To be bullish means to be optimistic about the future potential of the market.

capitalization-weighted A term typically used to describe a stock market index such as the S&P 500 where the price of each stock is multiplied by the number of shares outstanding to create an index that reflects the relative importance of a company in that index.

commercials A reference to large-scale commercial traders. An example would be large firms dealing in the grain trade, e.g., Cargill.

correction A movement in price opposite to that of the prevailing trend. During a bull market, a correction usually is thought to consist of a decline in prices. During a bear market, a correction usually is thought to consist of a rise in prices.

cycle A perceived, repetitious pattern in stock prices. Usually, a cycle is measured from what is perceived to be an important low price to another important low price. Cycles can be based on hourly, daily, weekly, monthly or yearly charts.

cycle extension When the market continues to move in the same direction, although cycle analysis suggests that the end of that move is imminent.

cycle inversion When the market moves strongly in a direction opposite to that predicted by cycle analysis.

day-traders people who buy and sell stocks within the same day. Rarely do they hold positions overnight.

discount rate The rate paid by banks that borrow money directly from the Federal Reserve System. It often is lower than the Treasury bill rate and substantially lower than the federal funds rate. Borrowing from the discount window, however, subjects banks to especially close scrutiny, and member banks would rather avoid borrowing from the Fed, if possible.

dummy variables Random factors introduced as supposedly independent variables into a regression equation that, in fact, have no causal relationship with the dependent variable. Their presence causes the R-squared to increase, which suggests that these variables have increased the percentage of the total variation in the equation and which is explained by the independent variables as a group. In reality, the R-squared has risen, but not the accuracy of the model.

intermediate term This term has no standard definition. For the day-trader, it might mean several hours. For the person who buys or sells over several days' or weeks' time, it might mean a few weeks. For someone who buys and sells stock every few months, it might mean one to three months. For someone who tends to hold on to stocks for years at a time, it might mean three to six months. In this book, it refers to one to three months.

investors Individuals who buy stocks, bonds or other financial instruments and hold them for long-term dividends, interest or capital appreciation. Usually, an investor does not buy and sell the same stocks, bonds, etc., on a daily, weekly or even monthly basis.

leverage Refers to the relationship between debt and equity. The greater the debt relative to equity, the greater the leverage. Those who buy stocks on margin are said to use leverage by virtue of the fact that they have to pay half of the value of the stock and can borrow the rest from their broker.

long To be long a stock is simply to buy a stock and hold it for an indefinite period.

long-term This term has no standard definition. For a day-trader, it might mean the entire day. For someone who buys and sells stocks every few days or weeks, it might mean a month or more. For someone who buys or sells stock every few months, it might mean a year or two. For someone who holds on to stocks for several years at a time, this might mean five years or more. In this book, it refers to a year or more.

margin The purchase of a financial instrument with a partial down payment financed through the borrowing of the rest of the money owed.

nesting of cycles   When several cycle bottoms coincide.

no-load funds   Funds that do not charge a sales commission or an exit fee. They are sold directly through the mutual fund company and usually are not available through brokers. Some brokerages, however, will charge a small transaction fee for buying and selling no-load mutual funds for their clients. This seems to defeat the purpose of buying these funds.

nominal cycles   Cycles based on average lengths of time.

open interest   Simply a measure of the total number of contracts in existence. Volume is simply a measure of the total number of transactions taking place. If, for example, a trader sells a futures contract in the market, open interest increases by one and volume increases by one. If that trader subsequently repurchases that contract, open interest drops by one, while volume increases by one.

option   The right to buy or sell something. Usually limited in terms of time, e.g., a 30-day option is the right to buy or sell something within the next 30 days.

overbought   Best defined as a condition created by excessive demand for a stock or commodity over a particular period. Such a condition suggests that the price of that stock or commodity is likely to sell off or go sideways for the immediate future.

oversold   A condition resulting from excessive supply of a stock or commodity over a particular period. Such a condition suggests that the price of that stock or commodity is likely to rally or go sideways for the immediate future.

position   A term used to refer to whether a trader or investor is long or short a stock or market.

premium   The price paid for an option.

price-dividend ratio   The price of a stock divided by the dividends it pays on an annual basis. For the market, the price-dividend ratio is the price of an index divided by the dividends paid by all stocks in that index.

price-earnings ratio   The price of a stock divided by the earnings of that company over the entire fiscal year. The price-earnings ratio of the stock market is the price of an index divided by the total earnings of all companies that make up that index.

price-to-book ratio   The price of a stock versus the book value of that company. The price-to-book value of a capitalization-weighted index is the price of all the stocks in an index multiplied by the total number of shares outstanding for each company divided by the book value of all companies in that index.

print high The actual high recorded for the day at any one instant and quite different from the theoretical high for the day, which is calculated by taking the highest prices for each stock for that day and adding them together. Unfortunately, the theoretical high most often is the one found in newspapers.

print low The actual low recorded for the day at any one instant and quite different from the theoretical low for the day, which is calculated by taking the lowest prices for each stock and adding them together. The theoretical low is the one most often found in most newspapers.

random noise An increase in the nonsystematic variation of a set of variables that does not add to the ability to predict the independent variable.

retail customers A popular euphemism for the general public.

reversal day A day on which a stock or index moves sharply higher (or lower) than the previous day and then changes direction abruptly. Quite often, during a rally, a reversal day sees the market open higher than the previous day's close and then close lower than the previous day's close. During a decline, a reversal day often sees the market open lower than the previous day's close and then close higher than the previous day's close.

risk-adjusted return Produced by recalculating total returns to take into account the volatility of that investment over time.

short To sell stock that you do not own. You borrow that stock from a brokerage, sell it in the market, pay interest on the value of the stock to the brokerage and are liable for all dividends paid on that stock. Eventually, you buy back that stock from the market and return it to the brokerage. If you sold it for more than it cost you to buy that stock back, you keep the difference as your profit. The repurchase of stock sold short is called covering your short.

short term There is no standard definition for short term. Day-traders would think that the short term is a few minutes. Those who buy and sell stocks every few weeks or months might regard the short term as a few days. Those who tend to hold the same stocks for a year or more might regard the short term as several weeks. In this book, we refer to the short term as one to three weeks.

simple moving average A simple moving average, or SMA, is computed by adding the data for weeks 1 through 13 and dividing by 13 for the first data point at week 13. Then, you drop week 1 and add week 14. You recompute the total for weeks 2 through 14 and divide by 13 again to get the data point for week 14, etc.

slippage The difference between the price at the time when a decision to buy or sell was made and the actual price of that trade.

trader Someone who buys and sells stock frequently and rarely holds the same stock for a year or more.

volatility Simply price fluctuation over time.

year over year Statistics created by dividing the current data by that released for the same period one year ago. Thus, for example, you divide the LEI data for December 1991 by the LEI data for December 1990 to get a year-over-year comparison.

year to date Statistics created the same way as year-over-year data.

Bibliography

Arms, Richard. *The Arms Index*. Homewood, Ill.: Dow Jones-Irwin, 1988.

Babcock, Bruce, Jr., *The Dow Jones-Irwin Guide to Trading Systems*. Homewood, Ill.: Dow Jones-Irwin, 1989.

Burke, Michael. *The All-New GUIDE to the Three-Point Reversal Method of Point and Figure Construction and Formations*. New Rochelle, N.Y.: Chartcraft, 1990.

Cardiff, Gray Emerson. *Panic-Proof Investing*. New York: Prentice-Hall, 1988.

Colby, Robert W., and Thomas A. Meyers. *The Encyclopedia of Technical Market Indicators*. Homewood, Ill.: Dow Jones-Irwin, 1988.

Crowell, Richard. *Stock Market Strategy*. New York: McGraw-Hill, 1977.

Dunnan, Nancy. *Dun and Bradstreet's Guide to Your Investments*. New York: Harper & Row, 1990.

Fosback, Norman. *Stock Market Logic*. Chicago: Dearborn Financial Publishing, 1991.

George, Wilfred R. *Tight Money Timing: The Impact of Interest Rates and the Federal Reserve on the Stock Market*. New York: Praeger, 1982.

Hayes, Michael. *The Dow Jones-Irwin Guide to Stock Market Cycles*. Homewood, Ill.: Dow Jones-Irwin, 1977.

Hulbert, Mark. *The Hulbert Guide to Financial Newsletters*. 4th ed. New York: New York Institute of Finance, 1990.

Individual Investor's Guide to Investment Publications. 1st ed. Chicago: International Pub. Corp., 1988.

Individual Investor's Guide to No-Load Mutual Funds. Chicago: International Pub. Corp., 1990.

Klingaman, William A. *1929: The Year of the Great Crash*. New York: Harper & Row, 1989.

Lefevre, Edwin. *Reminiscences of a Stock Operator*. Burlington, Vt.: Fraser Publishing, 1982.

Lewis, Michael. *Liar's Poker*. New York: Penguin, 1990.

Lynch, Peter. *One Up On Wall Street*. New York: Penguin, 1989.

McMillan, Lawrence G. *Options as a Strategic Investment: A Comprehensive Analysis of Listed Options Strategies*. New York: New York Institute of Finance, 1980.

Malkiel, Burton. *A Random Walk Down Wall Street*. New York: Norton, 1990.

Mamis, Justin. *How to Buy: an insider's guide to making money on the stock market*. New York: Farrar, Straus and Giroux, 1977.

_____. *When to Sell: inside strategies for stock market profits*. New York: Farrar, Straus and Giroux, 1977.

Murphy, John J. *Technical Analysis of the Futures Markets: A Comprehensive Guide to Trading Methods and Applications*. New York: New York Institute of Finance, 1986.

Nelson, Charles. *An Investor's Guide to Economic Indicators*. New York: Wiley & Sons, 1987.

Nison, Steve. *Japanese Candlestick Charting Techniques*. New York: New York Institute of Finance, 1991.

O'Neill, William J. *How To Make Money in Stocks: A Winning System in Good Times or Bad*. New York: McGraw-Hill, 1988.

Pring, Martin J. *Technical Analysis Explained*. New York: McGraw-Hill, 1985.

Rolo, Charles J. and Robert J. Klein, *Gaining on the Market: Your Complete Guide to Investment Strategy*. Boston: Little, Brown, 1988.

Schwager, Jack D. *Market Wizards: Interviews with Top Traders*. New York: HarperCollins, 1990.

Shimizu, Seiki. *The Japanese Chart of Charts*. Trans. Gregory S. Nicholson. Tokyo: Tokyo Futures Trading Publishing Co., 1986.

Touhey, John C. *Stock Market Forecasting for Alert Investors*. New York: AMACOM, 1980.

Weinstein, Stan. *Stan Weinstein's Secrets for Profiting in Bull and Bear Markets*. Homewood, Ill.: Dow Jones-Irwin, 1988.

Wilder, J. Welles, Jr. *New Concepts in Technical Trading Systems*. Greensboro, N.C.: Trend Research, 1978.

Yates, James. *The Options Strategy Spectrum*. Homewood, Ill.: Dow Jones-Irwin, 1987.

Zweig, Martin. *Winning on Wall Street*. New York: Warner, 1986.

Index